THE ALL-NIGHT VIGIL

for
CHOIR AND LAITY

Published with the blessing

of

His Eminence Archbishop Laurus

of

Syracuse and Holy Trinity

INTRODUCTORY NOTE

This All-Night Vigil book is a companion book to the Divine Liturgy book already published, and is the successor to the typewritten editions of 1979, 1984, and 1986. Like the Liturgy book, it owes many things to many sources, and some of the credits mentioned there apply here also. It is intended to help the worshipper at a Saturday night service as conducted in the Russian Church Abroad follow along step by step, and it contains many things from the unvarying portions of the service, as well as rubrics from many sources, to enable the worshipper to do just that.

The Psalter according to the Seventy, published by Holy Transfiguration Monastery, Brookline, Mass., is used throughout, wherever psalms and verses from the psalms are a part of the service.

This is not an official text of the Russian Church Abroad.

The Indiction, or Church New Year, 1993.

Rassaphor-monk Laurence

Revised Edition, Summer 1998

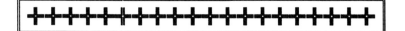

THE ALL-NIGHT VIGIL

THE GREAT VESPERS

Deacon (If there be no deacon, omit): Arise! O Lord, bless!

Priest: Glory to the holy, and consubstantial, and life-creating, and indivisible Trinity, always, now and ever, and unto the ages of ages.

CHOIR: Amen.

Clergy: O come, let us worship God our King.

O come, let us worship and fall down before Christ our King and God.

O come, let us worship and fall down before Christ Himself, our King and God.

O come, let us worship and fall down before Him.

Then the choir chanteth the following selected verses from the Introductory Psalm, i.e., the 103rd Psalm, while the priest censeth the church and the people:

Bless the Lord, O my soul. Blessed art Thou, O Lord. Bless the Lord, O my soul. O Lord my God, Thou hast been magnified exceedingly.

Refrain: Blessed art Thou, O Lord.

Confession and majesty hast Thou put on.

Refrain: Blessed art Thou, O Lord.

Upon the mountains shall the waters stand.

Refrain: Wondrous are Thy works, O Lord.

Between the mountains will the waters run.

Refrain: Wondrous are Thy works, O Lord.

In Wisdom hast Thou made them all, hast Thou made them all.

Refrain: Glory to Thee, O Lord, Who hast made them all, Who hast made them all.

Glory to the Father, and to the Son, and to the Holy Spirit.

Both now and ever, and unto the ages of ages. Amen.

Alleluia, alleluia, alleluia. Glory to Thee, O God. *Thrice.*

Then the deacon (priest) saith the Great Ectenia:

In peace let us pray to the Lord.

CHOIR: Lord, have mercy, *after each petition.*

For the peace from above, and the salvation of our souls, let us pray to the Lord.

For the peace of the whole world, the good estate of the holy churches of God, and the union of all, let us pray to the Lord.

For this holy temple, and for them that with faith, reverence, and the fear of God enter herein, let us pray to the Lord.

For the Orthodox episcopate of the Church of Russia; for our lord the Very Most Reverend Metropolitan *N.*, First Hierarch of the Russian Church Abroad; for our lord the Most Reverend (Archbishop *or* Bishop *N., whose diocese it is*); for the venerable priesthood, the diaconate in Christ, for all the clergy and people, let us pray to the Lord.

For the suffering Russian land and its Orthodox people both in the homeland and in the diaspora, and for their salvation, let us pray to the Lord.

For this land, its authorities and armed forces, let us pray to the Lord.

That He may deliver His people from enemies visible and invisible, and confirm in us oneness of mind, brotherly love, and piety, let us pray to the Lord.

For this city (*or* town, *or* holy monastery), every city and country, and the faithful that dwell therein, let us pray to the Lord.

For seasonable weather, abundance of the fruits of the earth, and peaceful times, let us pray to the Lord.

For travelers by sea, land, and air, for the sick, the suffering, the imprisoned, and for their salvation, let us pray to the Lord.

That we may be delivered from all tribulation, wrath, and necessity, let us pray to the Lord.

Help us, save us, have mercy on us, and keep us, O God, by Thy grace.

Calling to remembrance our most holy, most pure, most blessed, glorious Lady Theotokos and Ever-Virgin Mary with all the saints, let us commit ourselves and one another and all our life unto Christ our God.

CHOIR: To Thee, O Lord.

Priest: For unto Thee is due all glory, honour, and worship: to the Father, and to the Son, and to the Holy Spirit, now and ever, and unto the ages of ages.

CHOIR: Amen.

Then, if it be Saturday evening, the 1st Stasis of the 1st Kathisma is read, with the choir chanting the indicated verses. On feasts the chanted verses are usually the only verses of the kathisma appointed.

PSALM 1

Reader/Canonarch:

B lessed is the man that hath not walked in the counsel of the ungodly.

CHOIR: Blessed is the man that hath not walked in the counsel of the ungodly. Alleluia, alleluia, alleluia.

Reader: Nor stood in the way of sinners, nor sat in the seat of the pestilent. But his will is rather in the law of the Lord, and in His law will he meditate day and night. And he shall be like the tree which is planted by the streams of the waters, which shall bring forth its fruit in its season; and its leaf shall not fall, and all things whatsoever he may do shall prosper. Not so are the ungodly, not so; but rather they are like the chaff which the wind doth hurl away from the face of the earth. For this reason shall the ungodly not stand up in judgment, nor sinners in the council of the righteous. For the Lord knoweth the way of the righteous, and the way of the ungodly shall perish.

CHOIR: For the Lord knoweth the way of the righteous, and the way of the ungodly shall perish. Alleluia, alleluia, alleluia.

PSALM 2

Reader/Canonarch:

Why have the heathen raged, and the peoples meditated empty things? The kings of the earth were aroused, and the rulers were assembled together, against the Lord, and against His Christ. Let us break their bonds asunder, and let us cast away their yoke from us. He that dwelleth in the heavens shall laugh them to scorn, and the Lord shall deride them. Then shall He speak unto them in His wrath, and in His anger shall He trouble them. But as for Me, I was established as king by Him, upon Sion His holy mountain, proclaiming the commandment of the Lord. The Lord said unto Me: Thou art My Son, this day have I begotten Thee. Ask of Me, and I will give Thee the nations for Thine inheritance, and the uttermost parts of the earth for Thy possession. Thou shalt herd them with a rod of iron; Thou shalt shatter them like a potter's vessels. And now, O ye kings, understand; be instructed, all ye that judge the earth. Serve ye the Lord with fear, and rejoice in Him with trembling.

CHOIR: Serve ye the Lord with fear, and rejoice in Him with trembling. Alleluia, alleluia, alleluia.

Reader: Lay hold of instruction, lest at any time the Lord be angry, and ye perish from the righteous way. When quickly His wrath be kindled, blessed are all that have put their trust in Him.

CHOIR: Blessed are all that have put their trust in Him. Alleluia, alleluia, alleluia.

PSALM 3

Reader/Canonarch:

O Lord, why are they multiplied that afflict me? Many rise up against me. Many say unto my soul: There is no salvation for him in his God. But Thou, O Lord, art my helper, my glory, and the lifter up of my head. I cried unto the Lord with my voice, and He heard me out of His holy mountain. I laid me down and slept; I awoke, for the Lord will help me. I will not be afraid of ten thousands of people that set themselves against me round about. Arise, O Lord, save me, O my God.

CHOIR: Arise, O Lord, save me, O my God. Alleluia, alleluia, alleluia.

Reader: For Thou hast smitten all who without cause are mine enemies; the teeth of sinners hast Thou broken. Salvation is of the Lord, and Thy blessing is upon Thy people.

CHOIR: Salvation is of the Lord, and Thy blessing is upon Thy people. Alleluia, alleluia, alleluia.

Glory to the Father, and to the Son, and to the Holy Spirit, both now and ever, and unto the ages of ages. Amen. Alleluia, alleluia, alleluia.

Alleluia, alleluia, alleluia. Glory to Thee, O God. *Thrice.*

Deacon (Priest): Again and again, in peace let us pray to the Lord.

CHOIR: Lord, have mercy.

Deacon (Priest): Help us, save us, have mercy on us, and keep us, O God, by Thy grace.

CHOIR: Lord, have mercy.

Deacon (Priest): Calling to remembrance our most holy, most pure, most blessed, glorious Lady Theotokos and Ever-Virgin Mary with all the saints, let us commit ourselves and one another and all our life unto Christ our God.

CHOIR: To Thee, O Lord.

Priest: For Thine is the dominion, and Thine is the kingdom, and the power, and the glory: of the Father, and of the Son, and of the Holy Spirit, now and ever, and unto the ages of ages.

CHOIR: Amen.

Reader, 2nd Stasis of the 1st Kathisma:

PSALM 4

When I called upon Thee, O God of my righteousness, Thou didst hearken unto me; in mine affliction Thou hast enlarged me. Have compassion on me and hear my prayer. O ye sons of men, how long will ye be slow of heart? Why do ye love vanity, and seek after falsehood? Know also that the Lord hath made wondrous His holy one; the Lord will hearken unto me when I cry unto Him. Be angry, and sin not; feel compunction upon your beds for what ye say in your hearts. Sacrifice a sacrifice of righteousness, and hope in the Lord. Many say: Who will show unto us good things? The light of Thy countenance, O Lord, hath been signed upon us; Thou hast given gladness to my heart. From the fruit of their wheat, wine, and oil are they multiplied. In peace in the same place I shall lay me down and sleep. For Thou, O Lord, alone hast made me to dwell in hope.

PSALM 5

Unto my words give ear, O Lord; hear my cry. Attend unto the voice of my supplication, O my King and my God; for unto Thee will I pray, O Lord. In the morning Thou shalt hear my voice. In the morning shall I stand before Thee, and Thou shalt look upon me; for not a God that willest iniquity art Thou. He that worketh evil shall not dwell near Thee, nor shall transgressors abide before Thine eyes. Thou hast hated all them that work iniquity; Thou shalt destroy all them that speak a lie. A man that is bloody and deceitful shall the Lord abhor. But as for me, in the multitude of Thy mercy shall I go into Thy house; I shall worship toward Thy holy temple in fear of Thee. O Lord, guide me in the way of Thy righteousness; because of mine enemies, make straight my way before Thee. For in their mouth there is no truth; their heart is vain. Their throat is an open sepulchre, with their tongues have they spoken deceitfully; judge them, O God. Let them fall down on account of their own devisings; according to the multitude of their ungodliness, cast them out, for they have embittered Thee, O Lord. And let all them be glad that hope in Thee; they shall ever rejoice, and Thou shalt dwell among them. And all shall glory in Thee that love Thy name, for Thou shalt bless the righteous. O Lord, as with a shield of Thy good pleasure hast Thou crowned us.

PSALM 6

O Lord, rebuke me not in Thine anger, nor chasten me in Thy wrath. Have mercy on me, O Lord, for I am weak. Heal me, O Lord, for my bones are troubled, and my soul is troubled greatly; but Thou, O Lord, how long? Turn to me again, O Lord, deliver my soul; save me for Thy mercy's sake. For in death there is none that is mindful of Thee, and in hades who will confess Thee? I toiled in my groaning; every night I will wash my bed, with tears will I water my couch. Through wrath is mine eye become troubled, I have grown old among all mine enemies. Depart from me all ye that work vanity, for the Lord hath heard the voice of my weeping. The Lord hath heard my supplication, the Lord hath received my prayer. Let all mine enemies be greatly put to shame and be troubled, let them be turned back, and speedily be greatly put to shame.

Glory to the Father, and to the Son, and to the Holy Spirit, both now and ever, and unto the ages of ages. Amen.

Alleluia, alleluia, alleluia. Glory to Thee, O God. *Thrice.*

Deacon (Priest): Again and again, in peace let us pray to the Lord.

CHOIR: Lord, have mercy.

Deacon (Priest): Help us, save us, have mercy on us, and keep us, O God, by Thy grace.

CHOIR: Lord, have mercy.

Deacon (Priest): Calling to remembrance our most holy, most pure, most blessed, glorious Lady Theotokos and Ever-Virgin Mary with all the saints, let us commit ourselves and one another and all our life unto Christ our God.

CHOIR: To Thee, O Lord.

Priest: For a good God art Thou, and the Lover of mankind, and unto Thee do we send up glory: to the Father, and to the Son, and to the Holy Spirit, now and ever, and unto the ages of ages.

CHOIR: Amen.

Reader, 3rd Stasis of the 1st Kathisma:

PSALM 7

O Lord my God, in Thee have I put my hope; save me from them that persecute me, and do Thou deliver me. Lest at any time like a lion he seize my soul, when there is none to redeem me, nor to save. O Lord my God, if I have done this, if there be injustice in my hands, if I have paid back evil to them that rendered evil unto me, then let me fall back empty from mine enemies. Then let the enemy pursue my soul, and take it, and let him tread down my life into the earth, and my glory let him bring down into the dust. Arise, O Lord, in Thine anger, exalt Thyself to the furthest boundaries of Thine enemies. And arouse Thyself, O Lord my God, in the commandment which Thou hast enjoined, and a congregation of peoples shall surround Thee. And for their sakes return Thou on high. The Lord shall judge the peoples. Judge me, O Lord, according to my righteousness, and according to mine innocence within me. Let the wickedness of sinners be ended, and do Thou guide the righteous man, O God, that searchest out the hearts and reins. Righteous is my help from God, Who saveth them who are upright of heart. God is a judge that is righteous, strong and forbearing, and inflicteth not wrath every day. Unless ye be converted, His glittering sword shall He furbish; He hath bent His bow, and hath made it ready. And on it He hath made ready the instruments of death, His arrows for them that rage hotly hath He perfected. Behold, he was in travail with unrighteousness, he hath conceived toil and brought forth iniquity. He opened a pit and dug it, and he shall fall into the hole which he hath made. His toil shall return upon his own head, and upon his own pate shall his unrighteousness come down. I will give praise unto the Lord according to His righteousness, and I will chant unto the name of the Lord Most High.

PSALM 8

O Lord, our Lord, how wonderful is Thy name in all the earth! For Thy magnificence is lifted high above the heavens. Out of the mouths of babes and sucklings hast Thou perfected praise, because of Thine enemies, to destroy the enemy and avenger. For I will behold the heavens, the works of Thy fingers, the moon and the stars, which Thou hast founded. What is man, that Thou art mindful of him? Or the son of man, that Thou visitest him? Thou hast made him a little lower than the angels; with glory and honour hast Thou crowned him, and Thou hast set him over the works of Thy hands. All things hast Thou subjected under his feet, sheep, and all oxen, yea, and the beasts of the field, the birds of the air, and the fish of the sea, the things that pass through the paths of the sea. O Lord, our Lord, how wonderful is Thy name in all the earth!

Glory to the Father, and to the Son, and to the Holy Spirit, both now and ever, and unto the ages of ages. Amen.

Alleluia, alleluia, alleluia. Glory to Thee, O God. *Thrice.*

Deacon (Priest): Again and again, in peace let us pray to the Lord.

CHOIR: Lord, have mercy.

Deacon (Priest): Help us, save us, have mercy on us, and keep us, O God, by Thy grace.

CHOIR: Lord, have mercy.

Deacon (Priest): Calling to remembrance our most holy, most pure, most blessed, glorious Lady Theotokos and Ever-Virgin Mary with all the saints, let us commit ourselves and one another and all our life unto Christ our God.

CHOIR: To Thee, O Lord.

Priest: For Thou art our God, and unto Thee do we send up glory: to the Father, and to the Son, and to the Holy Spirit, now and ever, and unto the ages of ages.

CHOIR: Amen.

And immediately we chant: Lord, I have cried *(Psalms 140, 141, 129, 116) in the appointed tone.*

Reader/Canonarch: In the __ Tone: Lord, I have cried unto Thee, hearken unto me.

CHOIR:

Lord, I have cried unto Thee, hearken unto me.* Hearken unto me, O Lord.* Lord, I have cried unto Thee, hearken unto me;* attend to the voice of my supplication,* when I cry unto Thee.* Hearken unto me, O Lord.

Let my prayer be set forth* as incense before Thee,* the lifting up of my hands* as an evening sacrifice.* Hearken unto me, O Lord.

And the verses according to their order:

Set, O Lord, a watch before my mouth, and a door of enclosure round about my lips.

Incline not my heart unto words of evil, to make excuse with excuses in sins,

With men that work iniquity; and I will not join with their chosen.

The righteous man will chasten me with mercy and reprove me; as for the oil of the sinner, let it not anoint my head.

For yet more is my prayer in the presence of their pleasures; swallowed up near by the rock have their judges been.

They shall hear my words, for they be sweetened; as a clod of earth is broken upon the earth, so have their bones been scattered nigh unto hades.

For unto Thee, O Lord, O Lord, are mine eyes, in Thee have I hoped; take not my soul away.

Keep me from the snare which they have laid for me, and from the stumbling-blocks of them that work iniquity.

The sinners shall fall into their own net; I am alone until I pass by.

With my voice unto the Lord have I cried, with my voice unto the Lord have I made supplication.

I will pour out before Him my supplication, mine affliction before Him will I declare.

When my spirit was fainting within me, then Thou knewest my paths.

In this way wherein I have walked they hid for me a snare.

I looked upon my right hand, and beheld, and there was none that did know me.

Flight hath failed me, and there is none that watcheth out for my soul.

I have cried unto Thee, O Lord; I said: Thou art my hope, my portion art Thou in the land of the living.

Attend unto my supplication, for I am

brought very low.

Deliver me from them that persecute me, for they are stronger than I.

On Saturday evenings, 10 stichera are appointed.

Reader/Canonarch: Bring my soul out of prison: *CHOIR:* That I may confess Thy name. *And they chant the first sticheron.*

The righteous shall wait patiently for me* until Thou shalt reward me. *And the second sticheron.*

At feasts of the Lord which fall on Sundays, and vigils on other days, 8 stichera are appointed:

Out of the depths have I cried unto Thee, O Lord;* O Lord, hear my voice. *Sticheron.*

Let Thine ears be attentive* to the voice of my supplication. *Sticheron.*

If Thou shouldest mark iniquities, O Lord, O Lord, who shall stand?* For with Thee there is forgiveness. *Sticheron.*

For Thy name's sake have I patiently waited for Thee, O Lord; my soul hath waited patiently for Thy word,* my soul hath hoped in the Lord. *Sticheron.*

From the morning watch until night, from the morning watch* let Israel hope in the

Lord. *Sticheron.*

For with the Lord there is mercy, and with Him is plenteous redemption;* and He shall redeem Israel out of all his iniquities. *Sticheron.*

O praise the Lord, all ye nations;* praise Him all ye peoples. *Sticheron.*

For He hath made His mercy to prevail over us,* and the truth of the Lord abideth for ever. *Sticheron.*

Glory to the Father, and to the Son, and to the Holy Spirit. *Sticheron (Doxastichon) from the Menaion, if any. If not, continue with:*

Both now and ever, and unto the ages of ages. Amen. *Dogmatic Theotokion of the tone, or as appointed from the Menaion. Then, the Entry:*

Deacon (Priest): Wisdom! Aright!

CHOIR:

O Gentle Light of the holy glory of the immortal, heavenly, holy, blessed Father, O Jesus Christ: Having come to the setting of the sun, having beheld the evening light, we praise the Father, the Son, and the Holy Spirit: God. Meet it is for Thee at all times to be hymned with reverent voices, O Son of God, Giver of life. Wherefore, the world doth glorify Thee.

Deacon (Priest): Let us attend.

Priest: Peace be unto all.

Deacon (Priest): Wisdom! The Prokeimenon in the *(Saturday evenings)* 6th Tone: The Lord is King, He is clothed with majesty.

CHOIR: The Lord is King, He is clothed with majesty.

Deacon (Priest), stichos: The Lord is clothed with strength and He hath girt Himself.

CHOIR: The Lord is King...

Deacon (Priest), stichos: For He established the world which shall not be shaken.

CHOIR: The Lord is King...

Deacon (Priest), stichos: Holiness becometh Thy house, O Lord, unto length of days.

CHOIR: The Lord is King...

Deacon (Priest): The Lord is King:

CHOIR: He is clothed with majesty.

The Prokeimena for Vespers on Other Days

On Sunday evening, the 8th Tone:

Behold now, bless ye the Lord, all ye servants of the Lord.

Stichos: Ye that stand in the house of the Lord, in the courts of the house of our God.

On Monday evening, the 4th Tone:

The Lord will hearken unto me when I cry unto Him.

Stichos: When I called upon Thee, O God of my righteousness, Thou didst hearken unto me.

On Tuesday evening, the 1st Tone:

Thy mercy, O Lord, shall pursue me all the days of my life.

Stichos: The Lord is my shepherd, and I shall not want. In a place of green pasture, there hath He made me to dwell.

On Wednesday evening, the 5th Tone:

O God, in Thy name save me, and in Thy strength do Thou judge me.

Stichos: O God, hearken unto my prayer, give ear unto the words of my mouth.

On Thursday evening, the 6th Tone:

My help cometh from the Lord, Who hath made heaven and the earth.

Stichos: I have lifted up mine eyes to the mountains, from whence cometh my help.

On Friday evening, the 7th Tone:

O God, my helper art Thou, and Thy mercy shall go before me.

Stichos: Rescue me from mine enemies, O God, and from them that rise up against me redeem me.

And if there be parables (Old Testament readings),

before each reading:

Deacon (Priest): Wisdom!

Reader: The Reading is from ____ .

Deacon (Priest): Let us attend.

Then followeth the Augmented Ectenia:

Deacon (Priest): Let us say with our whole soul and with our whole mind, let us say.

CHOIR: Lord, have mercy.

Deacon (Priest): O Lord Almighty, the God of our fathers, we pray Thee, hearken and have mercy.

CHOIR: Lord, have mercy.

Deacon (Priest): Have mercy on us, O God, according to Thy great mercy, we pray Thee, hearken and have mercy.

CHOIR: Lord, have mercy. *Thrice. And likewise after the remaining petitions.*

Deacon (Priest): Again we pray for the Orthodox episcopate of the Church of Russia; for our lord the Very Most Reverend Metropolitan *N.*, First Hierarch of the Russian Church Abroad; for our lord the Most Reverend (Archbishop *or* Bishop *N., whose diocese it is*); and for all our brethren in Christ.

Again we pray for the suffering Russian

prayer to the Lord.

CHOIR: Lord, have mercy.

Deacon (Priest): Help us, save us, have mercy on us, and keep us, O God, by Thy grace.

CHOIR: Lord, have mercy.

Deacon (Priest): That the whole evening may be perfect, holy, peaceful, and sinless, let us ask of the Lord.

CHOIR: Grant this, O Lord. *And after the next five petitions.*

Deacon (Priest): An angel of peace, a faithful guide, a guardian of our souls and bodies, let us ask of the Lord.

Pardon and remission of our sins and offences, let us ask of the Lord.

Things good and profitable for our souls, and peace for the world, let us ask of the Lord.

That we may complete the remaining time of our life in peace and repentance, let us ask of the Lord.

A Christian ending to our life, painless, blameless, peaceful, and a good defence before the dread judgment seat of Christ, let us ask.

Calling to remembrance our most holy, most pure, most blessed, glorious Lady Theotokos and Ever-Virgin Mary with all the saints, let us commit ourselves and one another and all our life unto Christ our God.

CHOIR: To Thee, O Lord.

Priest: For a good God art Thou, and the Lover of mankind, and unto Thee do we send up glory: to the Father, and to the Son, and to the Holy Spirit, now and ever, and unto the ages of ages.

CHOIR: Amen.

Priest: Peace be unto all.

CHOIR: And to thy spirit.

Deacon (Priest): Let us bow our heads unto the Lord.

CHOIR: To Thee, O Lord.

Priest: Blessed and most glorified be the dominion of Thy kingdom: of the Father, and of the Son, and of the Holy Spirit, now and ever, and unto the ages of ages.

CHOIR: Amen. *Then, the Litia stichera are chanted as the clergy proceed to the narthex. If there be no Litia, the Aposticha stichera are chanted and the service continueth with* Now lettest Thou Thy servant depart, *page 36.*

Deacon (Priest):

Save, O God, Thy people, and bless Thine inheritance; visit Thy world with mercy and compassions; exalt the horn of Orthodox Christians, and send down upon us Thine abundant mercies: through the intercessions of our immaculate Lady Theotokos and Ever-Virgin Mary; through the power of the precious and life-giving Cross; through the mediations of the honourable, heavenly Bodiless Hosts; of the honourable, glorious Prophet, Forerunner, and Baptist John; of the holy, glorious, and all-praised apostles; (*if there be commemorated one of the Twelve Apostles or the Evangelists, there is said:* of the holy Apostle (and Evangelist) *N.*, and the other holy, glorious, and all-praised apostles); of our fathers among the saints and great ecumenical teachers and hierarchs: Basil the Great, Gregory the Theologian, and John Chrysostom; of our father among the saints, Nicholas the Wonderworker, archbishop of Myra in Lycia; of the holy Equals-of-the-Apostles Methodius and Cyril, Teachers of the Slavs; of the holy Right-believing and Equal-of-the-Apostles Great Prince Vladimir, and the Blessed Great Princess of

Russia Olga; of our fathers among the saints, the Wonderworkers of All Russia: Michael, Peter, Alexis, Jonah, Philip, Macarius, Demetrius, Metrophanes, Tikhon, Theodosius, Joasaph, Hermogenes, Pitirim, Innocent, and John; of the holy Hieromartyrs and Confessors: Tikhon, Patriarch of Moscow; Vladimir of Kiev, Benjamin and Joseph of Petrograd, Peter of Krutitsa, Cyril of Kazan, Agathangel of Yaroslavl; Andronicus of Perm, Hermogenes of Tobolsk, the priests John, John, Peter, and Philosoph, and all the new hieromartyrs and confessors of the Russian Church; of the holy, glorious, and victorious martyrs: the holy, glorious Great-martyr, Trophy-bearer, and Wonderworker George; the holy Great-martyr and Healer Panteleimon; the holy Great-martyr Barbara; and the holy Right-believing Russian Princes and Passion-bearers Boris and Gleb, and Igor; and the holy Right-believing Passion-bearers: Tsar-martyr Nicholas, Tsaritsa-martyr Alexandra, the Martyred Crown Prince Alexis, the Royal Martyrs Olga, Tatiana, Maria, and Anastasia; and the holy nun-martyrs: Grand Duchess Elizabeth and Nun Barbara, and all the New Martyrs of Russia; of our holy and God-bearing fathers Anthony and Theodosius of the Kiev Caves; Sergius, the Abbot of Radonezh, and Seraphim of Sarov; Job, Abbot and Wonderworker of Pochaev; of the holy Righteous John of Kronstadt; of the holy Blessed Xenia; of our holy and God-bearing fathers: Herman of Alaska; Paisius Velichkovsky; Leo, Macarius, Ambrose, and the other Elders of Optina; the hierarchs Innocent of Moscow, Nicholas of Japan, John of Shanghai and San Francisco; and Saint(s) *N.(N.), (whose temple it is and whose day it is)* whose memory we celebrate; of the holy and Righteous Ancestors of God Joachim and Anna; and of all the saints; we pray Thee, O Lord plenteous in mercy, hearken unto us sinners that pray unto Thee, and have mercy on us.

CHOIR: Lord, have mercy. *Forty times.*

Deacon (Priest): Again we pray for the Orthodox episcopate of the Church of Russia; for our lord the Very Most Reverend Metropolitan *N.*, First Hierarch of the Russian Church Abroad; for our lord the Most Reverend (Archbishop *or* Bishop *N., whose diocese it is*) (*if it be a monastery:* and for Archimandrite *N., or* our Abbot *N.*), and for all our brotherhood in Christ, and for every Christian soul that is oppressed and tormented, in need of the mercy and help of God; for the protection of this city (*or* town, *or* holy monastery) and them that dwell therein; for the peace and welfare of the whole world; for the good estate of the holy churches of God; for the salvation and help of our fathers and brethren that labour with zeal and the fear of God; for them that are absent and abroad; for the repose, refreshment, blessed memory, and remission of sins of all our fathers and brethren that have departed before us, and the Orthodox here and everywhere laid to rest; for the deliverance of the imprisoned; and for our brethren that are serving, and for all that serve and have served in this holy temple (*or* monastery), let us say:

CHOIR: Lord, have mercy. *Thirty times.*

Deacon (Priest): Again we pray for the suffering Russian land and its Orthodox people both in the homeland and in the diaspora, and for their salvation; and for this land, its authorities and armed forces, let us say:

CHOIR: Lord, have mercy. *Fifty times.*

Deacon (Priest): Again we pray that this city (*or* town), and this holy temple (*or* monastery), and every city and country may be preserved from famine, pestilence, earthquake, flood, fire, the sword, the invasion of aliens, and civil war; that our good and man-loving God may be gracious and favourable, that He may turn away all the wrath stirred up against us, and deliver us from His righteous threatening which hangeth over us, and have mercy on us.

CHOIR: Lord, have mercy. *Thrice.*

Deacon (Priest): Again we pray also that the Lord God may hearken unto the voice of the supplication of us sinners and have mercy on us.

CHOIR: Lord, have mercy. *Thrice.*

Priest (Bishop): Hearken unto us, O God our Saviour, Thou hope of all the ends of the earth and of them that be far off at sea; and be merciful, be merciful, O Master, regarding our sins, and have mercy on us; for a merciful God art Thou, and the Lover of mankind, and unto Thee do we send up glory: to the Father, and to the Son, and to the Holy Spirit, now and ever, and unto the ages of ages.

CHOIR: Amen.

Priest (Bishop): Peace be unto all.

CHOIR: And to thy spirit.

Deacon (Priest): Let us bow our heads unto the Lord.

CHOIR: To Thee, O Lord.

And as all bow their heads the priest (bishop) prayeth:

O Master plenteous in mercy, O Lord Jesus Christ our God: through the intercessions of our immaculate Lady Theotokos and Ever-Virgin Mary; through the power of the precious and life-giving Cross; through the mediations of the honourable, heavenly Bodiless Hosts; of the honourable, glorious Prophet, Forerunner, and Baptist John; of the holy, glorious, and all-praised apostles; of the holy, glorious, and victorious martyrs; of our holy and God-bearing fathers; of our fathers among the saints and great ecumenical teachers and hierarchs: Basil the Great, Gregory the Theologian, and John Chrysostom; of our father among the saints, Nicholas the Wonderworker, archbishop of Myra in Lycia; of the holy Equals-of-the-

Apostles Methodius and Cyril, Teachers of the Slavs; of the holy Right-believing and Equal-of-the-Apostles Great Prince Vladimir, and the Blessed Great Princess of Russia Olga; of our fathers among the saints, the Wonderworkers of all Russia: Michael, Peter, Alexis, Jonah, Philip, Macarius, Demetrius, Metrophanes, Tikhon, Theodosius, Joasaph, Hermogenes, Pitirim, Innocent, and John; of the holy Hiero-martyrs and Confessors: Tikhon, Patriarch of Moscow; Vladimir of Kiev, Benjamin and Joseph of Petrograd, Peter of Krutitsa, Cyril of Kazan, Agathangel of Yaroslavl, Andronicus of Perm, Hermogenes of Tobolsk, the priests John, John, Peter, and Philosoph, and all the new hieromartyrs and confessors of the Rus-sian Church; of the holy, glorious, and victori-ous martyrs: the holy, glorious Great-martyr, Trophy-bearer, and Wonderworker George; the holy Great-martyr and Healer Panteleimon; the holy Great-martyr Barbara; and the holy Right-believing Russian Princes and Passion-bearers Boris and Gleb, and Igor; and the holy Passion-bearers: Tsar-martyr Nicholas, Tsaritsa-martyr Alexandra, the Martyred Crown Prince

Alexis, and the Royal Martyrs Olga, Tatiana, Maria, and Anastasia; and the holy nun-martyrs: Grand Duchess Elizabeth and Nun Barbara, and all the New Martyrs of Russia; of our holy and God-bearing fathers Anthony and Theodosius of the Kiev Caves; Sergius, Abbot of Radonezh, and Seraphim of Sarov; Job, Abbot and Wonderworker of Pochaev; of the holy Righteous John of Kronstadt; of the holy Blessed Xenia; of our holy and God-bearing fathers: Herman of Alaska; Paisius Velichkovsky; Leo, Macarius, Ambrose, and the other Elders of Optina; the hierarchs: Innocent of Moscow, Nicholas of Japan, and John of Shanghai and San Francisco; of Saint(s) *N. (N.)*, *(whose temple it is and whose day it is)* whose memory we celebrate; of the holy and Righteous Ancestors of God Joachim and Anna; and of all Thy saints: make our prayer acceptable; grant us the remission of our sins; shelter us with the shelter of Thy wings; drive away from us every enemy and adversary; make our life peaceful, O Lord; have mercy on us and on Thy world, and save our souls, for Thou art good and the Lover of mankind.

CHOIR: Amen.

Then, chanting the stichera of the Aposticha, we enter the temple. After the Theotokion, the Prayer of St. Symeon the God-receiver is said by the canonarch:

Now lettest Thou Thy servant depart in peace, O Master, according to Thy word, for mine eyes have seen Thy salvation, which Thou hast prepared before the face of all peoples; a light of revelation for the Gentiles, and the glory of Thy people Israel.

Reader: Holy God, Holy Mighty, Holy Immortal, have mercy on us. *Thrice.*

Glory to the Father, and to the Son, and to the Holy Spirit, both now and ever, and unto the ages of ages. Amen.

O most holy Trinity, have mercy on us. O Lord, blot out our sins. O Master, pardon our iniquities. O Holy One, visit and heal our infirmities for Thy name's sake.

Lord, have mercy. *Thrice.*

Glory to the Father, and to the Son, and to the Holy Spirit, both now and ever, and unto the ages of ages. Amen.

Our Father, Who art in the heavens, hallowed be Thy name. Thy kingdom come, Thy will be done, on earth as it is in heaven. Give us this day our daily bread; and forgive us our debts, as we forgive our debtors; and lead us not into temptation, but deliver us from the evil one.

Priest (Bishop): For Thine is the kingdom, and the power, and the glory: of the Father, and of the Son, and of the Holy Spirit, now and ever, and unto the ages of ages.

CHOIR: Amen.

Then, we chant the Dismissal Troparion. If it be a regular Sunday Vigil without a Litia, we chant O Theotokos and Virgin, rejoice, *thrice. If it be one of the Twelve Feasts, we chant the troparion of the feast thrice. If it be some other vigil coinciding with a Sunday, we chant* O Theotokos and Virgin, *twice, and the troparion of the feast once; if it be not a Sunday, we chant the troparion of the feast twice, and* O Theotokos and Virgin, *once.*

O Theotokos and Virgin, rejoice!* Mary, full of grace, the Lord is with thee;* blessed art thou among women,* and blessed is the Fruit of thy womb;* for thou hast borne the Saviour of our souls.

Then, if there hath been a Litia, the blessing of

the loaves, wheat, wine, and oil:

Deacon (Priest): Let us pray to the Lord.

CHOIR: Lord, have mercy.

Priest (Bishop):

O Lord Jesus Christ our God, Who didst bless the five loaves and didst satisfy the five thousand: Do Thou Thyself bless also these loaves, wheat, wine, and oil; and multiply them in this city (*or* town, *or* holy monastery) and in all Thy world; and sanctify the faithful that partake of them. For it is Thou Who dost bless and sanctify all things, O Christ our God, and unto Thee do we send up glory, together with Thine unoriginate Father, and Thine All-holy and good and life-creating Spirit, now and ever, and unto the ages of ages.

CHOIR: Amen. *And immediately:* Blessed be the name of the Lord from henceforth and for evermore. *Thrice.*

And the first ten verses of the 33rd Psalm:

I will bless the Lord at all times,* His praise shall continually be in my mouth.

In the Lord shall my soul be praised;* let the meek hear and be glad.

O magnify the Lord with me,* and let us

exalt His name together,

I sought the Lord, and He heard me,* and delivered me from all my tribulations.

Come unto Him, and be enlightened,* and your faces shall not be ashamed.

This poor man cried, and the Lord heard him,* and saved him out of all his tribulations.

The angel of the Lord will encamp round about them that fear Him,* and will deliver them.

O taste and see that the Lord is good;* blessed is the man that hopeth in Him.

O fear the Lord, all ye His saints;* for there is no want to them that fear Him.

Rich men have turned poor and gone hungry;* but they that seek the Lord shall not be deprived of any good thing.

Priest (Bishop): The blessing of the Lord be upon you, through His grace and love for mankind, always, now and ever, and unto the ages of ages.

CHOIR: Amen.

THE END OF GREAT VESPERS

❈❈❈❈❈❈❈

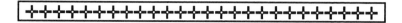

The Matins

The Six Psalms

We begin Matins with the Six Psalms, listening in silence and with compunction (standing, with no moving about). And the reader, with reverence and fear of God, saith:

Glory to God in the highest, and on earth peace, good will among men. *Thrice.(And we make the sign of the Cross and bow thrice.)*

O Lord, Thou shalt open my lips, and my mouth shall declare Thy praise. *Twice.*

PSALM 3

O Lord, why are they multiplied that afflict me? Many rise up against me. Many say unto my soul: There is no salvation for him in his God. But Thou, O Lord, art my helper, my glory, and the lifter up of my head. I cried unto the Lord with my voice, and He heard me out of His holy mountain. I laid me down and slept; I awoke, for the Lord will help me. I will not be afraid of ten thousands of people that set themselves against me round about.

Arise, O Lord, save me, O my God, for Thou hast smitten all who without cause are mine enemies; the teeth of sinners hast Thou broken. Salvation is of the Lord, and Thy blessing is upon Thy people.

I laid me down and slept; I awoke, for the Lord will help me.

PSALM 37

O Lord, rebuke me not in Thine anger, nor chasten me in Thy wrath. For Thine arrows are fastened in me, and Thou hast laid Thy hand heavily upon me. There is no healing in my flesh in the face of Thy wrath; and there is no peace in my bones in the face of my sins. For mine iniquities are risen higher than my head; as a heavy burden have they pressed heavily upon me. My bruises are become noisome and corrupt in the face of my folly. I have been wretched and utterly bowed down until the end; all the day long I went with downcast face. For my loins are filled with mockings, and there is no healing in my flesh. I am afflicted and humbled exceedingly, I have roared from the groaning of my heart. O Lord, before Thee is all my desire, and my groaning is not hid from Thee. My heart is troubled, my strength hath failed me; and the light of mine eyes, even this is not with me. My friends and my neighbours drew nigh over against me and stood, and my nearest of kin stood afar off. And they that sought after my soul used violence; and they that sought evils for me spake vain things, and craftinesses all the day long did they meditate. But as for me, like a deaf man I heard them not, and was as a speechless man that openeth not his mouth. And I became as a man that heareth not, and that hath in his mouth no reproofs. For in Thee have I hoped, O Lord; Thou wilt hearken unto me, O Lord my God. For I said: Let never mine enemies rejoice over me; yea, when my feet were shaken, those men spake boastful words against me. For I am ready for scourges, and my sorrow is continually before me. For I will declare mine iniquity, and I will take heed concerning my sin. But mine enemies live and are made stronger than I, and they that hated me unjustly are multiplied. They that render me evil for good slandered me, because I pursued goodness. Forsake me

not, O Lord my God, depart not from me. Be
attentive unto my help, O Lord of my salvation.

Forsake me not, O Lord my God, depart
not from me. Be attentive unto my help, O
Lord of my salvation.

PSALM 62

O God, my God, unto Thee I arise early at
dawn. My soul hath thirsted for Thee;
how often hath my flesh longed after Thee in
a land barren and untrodden and unwatered.
So in the sanctuary have I appeared before
Thee to see Thy power and Thy glory, for Thy
mercy is better than lives; my lips shall praise
Thee. So shall I bless Thee in my life, and in
Thy name will I lift up my hands. As with mar-
row and fatness let my soul be filled, and with
lips of rejoicing shall my mouth praise Thee.
If I remembered Thee on my bed, at the dawn
I meditated on Thee. For Thou art become
my helper; in the shelter of Thy wings will I
rejoice. My soul hath cleaved after Thee, Thy
right hand hath been quick to help me. But as
for these, in vain have they sought after my
soul; they shall go into the nethermost parts of

the earth, they shall be surrendered unto the edge of the sword; portions for foxes shall they be. But the king shall be glad in God, everyone shall be praised that sweareth by Him; for the mouth of them is stopped that speak unjust things.

At the dawn I meditated on Thee. For Thou art become my helper; in the shelter of Thy wings will I rejoice. My soul hath cleaved after Thee, Thy right hand hath been quick to help me.

Glory to the Father, and to the Son, and to the Holy Spirit, both now and ever, and unto the ages of ages. Amen.

Alleluia, alleluia, alleluia. Glory to Thee, O God. *Thrice, with the sign of the Cross, but without bows.*

Lord, have mercy. *Thrice.*

Glory to the Father, and to the Son, and to the Holy Spirit, both now and ever, and unto the ages of ages. Amen.

PSALM 87

O Lord God of my salvation, by day have I cried and by night before Thee. Let my prayer come before Thee, bow down Thine ear unto my supplication. For filled with evils is my soul, and my life unto hades hath drawn nigh. I am counted with them that go down into the pit; I am become as a man without help, free among the dead, like the bodies of the slain that sleep in the grave, whom Thou rememberest no more, and they are cut off from Thy hand. They laid me in the lowest pit, in darkness and in the shadow of death. Against me is Thine anger made strong, and all Thy billows hast Thou brought upon me. Thou hast removed my friends afar from me; they have made me an abomination unto themselves. I have been delivered up, and have not come forth; mine eyes are grown weak from poverty. I have cried unto Thee, O Lord, the whole day long; I have stretched out my hands unto Thee. Nay, for the dead wilt Thou work wonders? Or shall physicians raise them up that they may give thanks unto Thee? Nay, shall any in the grave tell of Thy mercy, and of Thy truth in that destruction? Nay, shall Thy wonders be known in that darkness, and Thy righteousness in that land that is forgotten? But as for me, unto Thee, O Lord, have I cried; and in the morning shall my prayer come before Thee. Wherefore, O Lord, dost Thou cast off my soul and turnest Thy face away from me? A poor man am I, and in troubles from my youth; yea, having been exalted, I was humbled and brought to distress. Thy furies have passed upon me, and Thy terrors have sorely troubled me. They came round about me like water, all the day long they compassed me about together. Thou hast removed afar from me friend and neighbour, and mine acquaintances because of my misery.

O Lord God of my salvation, by day have I cried and by night before Thee. Let my prayer come before Thee, bow down Thine ear unto my supplication.

PSALM 102

B less the Lord, O my soul, and all that is within me bless His holy name. Bless the Lord, O my soul, and forget not all that He hath done for thee, Who is gracious unto all thine iniquities, Who healeth all thine infirmities, Who redeemeth thy life from corruption, Who crowneth thee with mercy and compassion, Who fulfilleth thy desire with good things;

thy youth shall be renewed as the eagle's. The Lord performeth deeds of mercy, and executeth judgment for all them that are wronged. He hath made His ways known unto Moses, unto the sons of Israel the things that He hath willed. Compassionate and merciful is the Lord, long-suffering and plenteous in mercy; not unto the end will He be angered, neither unto eternity will He be wroth. Not according to our iniquities hath He dealt with us, neither according to our sins hath He rewarded us. For according to the height of heaven from the earth, the Lord hath made His mercy to prevail over them that fear Him. As far as the east is from the west, so far hath He removed our iniquities from us. Like as a father hath compassion upon His sons, so hath the Lord had compassion upon them that fear Him; for He knoweth whereof we are made, He hath remembered that we are dust. As for man, his days are as the grass; as a flower of the field, so shall he blossom forth. For when the wind is passed over it, then it shall be gone, and no longer will it know the place thereof. But the mercy of the Lord is from eternity, even unto eternity, upon them that fear Him. And His righteousness is upon sons of sons, upon them that keep His testament and remember His commandments to do them. The Lord in heaven hath prepared His throne, and His kingdom ruleth over all. Bless the Lord, all ye His angels, mighty in strength, that perform His word, to hear the voice of His words. Bless the Lord, all ye His hosts, His ministers that do His will. Bless the Lord, all ye His works, in every place of His dominion. Bless the Lord, O my soul

In every place of His dominion, bless the Lord, O my soul.

PSALM 142

O Lord, hear my prayer, give ear unto my supplication in Thy truth; hearken unto me in Thy righteousness. And enter not into judgment with Thy servant, for in Thy sight shall no man living be justified. For the enemy hath persecuted my soul; he hath humbled my life down to the earth. He hath sat me in darkness as those that have been long dead, and my spirit within me is become despondent; within me my heart is troubled. I remembered days of old, I meditated on all Thy works, I pondered on the creations of Thy hands. I stretched forth my hands unto Thee; my soul thirsteth after Thee like a waterless land. Quickly hear me, O Lord; my spirit hath fainted away. Turn not Thy face away from me, lest I be like unto them that go down into the pit. Cause me to hear Thy mercy in the morning; for in Thee have I put my hope. Cause me to know, O Lord, the way wherein I should walk; for unto Thee have I lifted up my soul. Rescue me from mine enemies, O Lord; unto Thee have I fled for refuge. Teach me to do Thy will, for Thou art my God. Thy good Spirit shall lead me in the land of uprightness; for Thy name's sake, O Lord, shalt Thou quicken me. In Thy righteousness shalt Thou bring my soul out of affliction, and in Thy mercy shalt Thou utterly destroy mine enemies. And Thou shalt cut off all them that afflict my soul, for I am Thy servant.

Hearken unto me, O Lord, in Thy righteousness, and enter not into judgment with Thy servant. *Twice.*

Thy good Spirit shall lead me in the land

of uprightness.

Glory to the Father, and to the Son, and to the Holy Spirit, both now and ever, and unto the ages of ages. Amen.

Alleluia, alleluia, alleluia. Glory to Thee, O God. *Thrice, with the sign of the Cross and a bow each time.*

Then the deacon (priest) saith the Great Ectenia:
In peace let us pray to the Lord.

CHOIR: Lord, have mercy, *after each petition.*

For the peace from above, and the salvation of our souls, let us pray to the Lord.

For the peace of the whole world, the good estate of the holy churches of God and the union of all, let us pray to the Lord.

For this holy temple, and for them that with faith, reverence, and the fear of God enter herein, let us pray to the Lord.

For the Orthodox episcopate of the Church of Russia; for our lord the Very Most Reverend Metropolitan *N.*, First Hierarch of the Russian Church Abroad; for our lord the Most Reverend (Archbishop *or* Bishop *N., whose diocese it is*); for the venerable priesthood, the diaconate in Christ, for all the clergy and people, let us pray to the Lord.

For the suffering Russian land and its Orthodox people both in the homeland and in the diaspora, and for their salvation, let us pray to the Lord.

For this land, its authorities and armed forces, let us pray to the Lord.

That He may deliver His people from enemies visible and invisible, and confirm in us oneness of mind, brotherly love, and piety, let us pray to the Lord.

For this city (*or* town, *or* holy monastery), every city and country, and the faithful that dwell therein, let us pray to the Lord.

For seasonable weather, abundance of the fruits of the earth, and peaceful times, let us pray to the Lord.

For travelers by sea, land, and air, for the sick, the suffering, the imprisoned, and for their salvation, let us pray to the Lord.

That we may be delivered from all tribulation, wrath, and necessity, let us pray to the Lord.

Help us, save us, have mercy on us, and

keep us, O God, by Thy grace.

Calling to remembrance our most holy, most pure, most blessed, glorious Lady Theotokos and Ever-Virgin Mary with all the saints, let us commit ourselves and one another and all our life unto Christ our God.

CHOIR: To Thee, O Lord.

Priest: For unto Thee is due all glory, honour, and worship: to the Father, and to the Son, and to the Holy Spirit, now and ever, and unto the ages of ages.

CHOIR: Amen.

Deacon (Priest): In the ___ Tone: God is the Lord and hath appeared unto us. Blessed is he that cometh in the name of the Lord.

Stichos 1: O give thanks unto the Lord, for He is good, for His mercy endureth for ever.

CHOIR: God is the Lord and hath appeared unto us. Blessed is he that cometh in the name of the Lord. *Chanted after each stichos.*

Stichos 2: Surrounding me they compassed me, and by the name of the Lord I warded them off.

Stichos 3: I shall not die, but live, and I shall tell of the works of the Lord.

Stichos 4: The stone which the builders rejected, the same is become the head of the corner. This is the Lord's doing, and it is marvelous in our eyes.

If it be a Sunday, and none of the Twelve Feasts happen to coincide with it, we chant the Troparion of the Resurrection of the proper tone, as given below, twice; then Glory: *troparion of the saint;* Both now: *the Theotokion for Sunday in the tone of the saint's troparion.*

If it be the feast of the Exaltation of the Cross, or of the Nativity of Christ, or Theophany, or Transfiguration, then, regardless of the day of the week, we chant the troparion of the feast twice; Glory. Both now: *and again the troparion of the feast.*

If a feast of the Theotokos fall on a Sunday, we chant the Sunday troparion of the tone twice; Glory. Both now: *and the troparion of the feast. If a feast of the Theotokos fall on some other day, the sequence is the same as for a feast of the Lord (i.e., a Theotokion is not used after the troparion on any feast of the Lord or the Theotokos).*

If a saint's feast of vigil rank fall on a Sunday, the sequence is the same as in the first paragraph of rubrics above. If it fall on some other day, we chant the troparion twice; Glory. Both now: *and the Sunday Theotokion in the tone of the Troparion.*

The Sunday (Resurrectional) Troparia of the Eight Tones:

1st Tone: When the stone had been sealed by the Jews,* and the soldiers were guarding Thine immaculate Body,* Thou didst rise on the third day, O Saviour,* granting life unto the world.* Wherefore, the Hosts of the heavens cried out to Thee, O Life-giver:* Glory to Thy Resurrection, O Christ.* Glory to Thy kingdom.* Glory to Thy dispensation, O only Lover of mankind.

2nd Tone: When Thou didst descend unto death, O Life Immortal,* then didst Thou slay hades with the lightning of Thy Divinity.* And when Thou didst also raise the dead out of the nethermost depths,* all the Hosts of the heavens cried out:* O Life-giver, Christ our God, glory be to Thee.

3rd Tone: Let the heavens be glad; let earthly things rejoice;* for the Lord hath wrought might with His arm.* He hath trampled down death by death;* the first-born of the dead hath He become.* From the belly of hades hath He delivered us* and hath granted to the world great mercy.

4th Tone: Having learned the joyful proclamation of the Resurrection from the angel,* and having cast off the ancestral condemnation,* the women disciples of the Lord* spake to the apostles exultantly:* Death is despoiled* and Christ God is risen,* granting to the world great mercy.

5th Tone: Let us, O faithful, praise and worship the Word* Who is co-unoriginate with the Father and the Spirit,* and Who was born of the Virgin for our salvation;* for He was pleased to ascend the Cross in the flesh* and to endure death,* and to raise the dead by His glorious Resurrection.

6th Tone: Angelic hosts were above Thy tomb,* and they that guarded Thee became as dead.* And Mary stood by the grave seeking Thine immaculate Body.* Thou didst despoil hades and wast not tempted by it.* Thou didst meet the Virgin and didst grant us life.* O Thou Who didst rise from the dead, O Lord, glory be to Thee.

7th Tone: Thou didst destroy death by Thy Cross,* Thou didst open paradise to the thief.* Thou didst change the lamentation of the

raise me up from the gates of death, that I may declare all Thy praises in the gates of the daughter of Sion. We will rejoice in Thy salvation. The heathen are ensnared in the destruction which they have wrought; in this snare which they hid hath their foot been caught. The Lord is known by the judgments which He executeth; in the works of his own hands hath the sinner been caught. Let sinners be turned away unto hades, yea, all the nations that are forgetful of God. For the poor man shall not be forgotten to the end; the patience of the paupers shall not perish for ever. Arise, O Lord, let not man prevail; let the nations be judged before Thee. O Lord, set a lawgiver over them; let the heathen know that they are but men. Why, O Lord, hast Thou gone to stand afar off? Why dost Thou overlook us in times of well-being and in afflictions? When the ungodly man is arrogant, the poor man burneth within; they are caught in the counsels which they devise. For the sinner praiseth himself in the lusts of his soul, and the unrighteous man likewise blesseth himself therein. The sinner hath provoked the Lord; according to the magnitude of his wrath, he careth not; God is not before him. Profane are his ways in every season, Thy judgments are removed from his sight, over all his enemies shall he gain dominion. For he said in his heart: I shall not be shaken; from generation to generation shall I be without harm. With cursing is his mouth filled, and with bitterness and deceit; under his tongue are toil and travail. He sitteth in ambush with the rich in secret places, that he may slay the innocent; his eyes are set upon the poor man. He lieth in wait in a secret place like a lion in his den; he lieth in wait to seize upon the poor man, to seize upon the poor man when he draweth him in. In his snare will he humble himself, he will bow down and fall while gaining dominion over the poor. For he said in his heart: God hath forgotten; He hath turned away His face, that He might not see unto the end. Arise, O Lord my God, let Thy hand be lifted high; forget not Thy paupers to the end. Why hath the ungodly one provoked God? For he hath said in his heart: He will not make enquiry. Thou seest, for Thou understandest travail and anger, that Thou mightest deliver him into Thy hands. To Thee hath the beggar been abandoned; for the orphan art Thou a helper. Break Thou the arm of the sinner and of the evil man; his sin shall be sought out and be found no more. The Lord shall be king for ever, and unto the ages of ages. Ye heathen shall perish out of His land. The desire of the poor hast Thou heard, O Lord; to the preparation of their heart hath Thine ear been attentive, to judge for the orphan and the humble, that man may no more presume to be haughty upon the earth.

PSALM 10

In the Lord have I hoped; how will ye say to my soul: Flee unto the mountains like a sparrow? For behold, the sinners have bent their bow, they have prepared arrows for the quiver, to shoot down in a moonless night the upright of heart. For what Thou hast formed they have destroyed; and the righteous man, what hath he done? The Lord is in His holy temple; the Lord, in heaven is His throne; His eyes are set upon the poor man, His eyelids examine the sons of men. The Lord examineth the righteous man and the ungodly; but he that loveth unrighteousness hateth his own soul. He will rain down snares upon sinners; fire and brimstone and wind of tempest shall be the portion of their cup. For the Lord is righteous and hath loved righteousness; upon uprightness hath His countenance looked.

Glory to the Father, and to the Son, and to the Holy Spirit.

CHOIR: Both now and ever, and unto the ages of ages. Amen.

Alleluia, alleluia, alleluia. Glory to Thee, O God. *Thrice.* Lord, have mercy. *Thrice.*

Glory to the Father, and to the Son, and to the Holy Spirit.

Reader: Both now and ever, and unto the ages of ages. Amen.

PSALM 11

Save me, O Lord, for a righteous man there is no more; for truths have diminished from the sons of men. Vain things hath each man spoken to his neighbour; deceitful lips are in his heart, and in his heart hath he spoken evils. Let the Lord destroy all deceitful lips and the tongue that speaketh boastful words, which have said: Our tongue will we magnify, our lips are our own. Who is lord over us? Because of the distress of the beggars and the groaning of the poor, now will I arise, saith the Lord; I will establish them in salvation, I will be manifest therein. The words of the Lord are pure words, silver that is fired, tried in the earth, brought to sevenfold purity. Thou, O Lord, shalt keep us and shalt preserve us from this generation, and for evermore. The ungodly walk round about; to the measure of Thy loftiness hast Thou esteemed the sons of men.

PSALM 12

How long, O Lord, wilt Thou utterly forget me? How long wilt Thou turn Thy face away from me? How long shall I take counsel in my soul with grievings in my heart by day and by night? How long shall mine enemy be exalted over me? Look upon me, hear me, O Lord my God; enlighten mine eyes, lest at any time I sleep unto death. Lest at any time mine enemy say: I have prevailed against him. They that afflict me will rejoice if I am shaken; but as for me, I have hoped in Thy mercy. My heart will rejoice in Thy salvation. I will sing unto the Lord, Who is my benefactor, and I will chant unto the name of the Lord Most High.

PSALM 13

The fool hath said in his heart: There is no God. They are become corrupt and loathsome in their ways; there is none that doeth good, no not one. The Lord looked down from heaven upon the sons of men, to see if there be any that understand or seek after God. They are all gone astray, they are altogether rendered useless, there is none that doeth good, no not one. Shall not all they that work iniquity come to understanding? They that eat up my people as They eat bread have not called upon the Lord. There have they feared with fear where there is no fear; for the Lord is in the generation of the righteous. The counsel of the poor man have ye shamed, but the Lord is his hope. Who shall give out of Sion the salvation of Israel? When the Lord hath turned back the captivity of His people, Jacob shall rejoice and Israel shall be glad.

Glory to the Father, and to the Son, and to the Holy Spirit.

CHOIR: Both now and ever, and unto the

ages of ages. Amen.

Alleluia, alleluia, alleluia. Glory to Thee, O God. *Thrice.* Lord, have mercy. *Thrice.*

Glory to the Father, and to the Son, and to the Holy Spirit.

Reader: Both now and ever, and unto the ages of ages. Amen.

PSALM 14

O Lord, who shall abide in Thy tabernacle? and who shall dwell in Thy holy mountain? He that walketh blameless and worketh righteousness, speaking truth in his heart, who hath not spoken deceitfully with his tongue, neither hath done evil to his neighbour, nor taken up a reproach against those near him. In his sight he that worketh evil is set at nought, but he glorifieth them that fear the Lord. He giveth oath to his neighbour, and forsweareth not. He hath not lent his money on usury, and hath not received bribes against the innocent. He that doeth these things shall never be shaken.

Psalm 15

Keep me, O Lord, for in Thee have I hoped. I said unto the Lord: Thou art my Lord;

for of my goods, no need hast Thou. In the saints that are in His earth hath the Lord been wondrous; He hath wrought all His desires in them. Their infirmities increased; thereupon they hastened. (*Diapsalm*) I will not assemble their assemblies of blood, nor will I make remembrance of their names through my lips. The Lord is the portion of mine inheritance and of my cup. Thou art He that restorest mine inheritance unto me. Portions have fallen to me that are among the best, for mine inheritance is most excellent to me. I will bless the Lord Who hath given me understanding; moreover, even till night have my reins instructed me. I beheld the Lord ever before me, for He is at my right hand, that I might not be shaken. Therefore did my heart rejoice and my tongue was glad; moreover, my flesh shall dwell in hope. For Thou wilt not abandon my soul in hades, nor wilt Thou suffer Thy Holy One to see corruption. Thou hast made known to me the ways of life, Thou wilt fill me with gladness with Thy countenance; delights are in Thy right hand for ever.

PSALM 16

Hearken, O Lord, unto my righteousness, attend unto my supplication. Give ear unto my prayer, which cometh not from deceitful lips. From before Thy face let my judgment come forth, let mine eyes behold uprightness. Thou hast proved my heart, Thou hast visited it in the night, Thou hast tried me by fire, and unrighteousness was not found in me. That my mouth might not speak of the works of men, for the sake of the words of Thy lips have I kept the ways that are hard. Set my footsteps in Thy paths, that my steps may not be shaken. I have cried for Thou hast hearkened unto me, O God. Incline Thine ear unto me, and hearken unto my words. Let Thy mercies be made wonderful, O Thou that savest them that hope in Thee. From them that have resisted Thy right hand, keep me, O Lord, as the apple of Thine eye. In the shelter of Thy wings wilt Thou shelter me, from the face of the ungodly which have oppressed me. Mine enemies have surrounded my soul, they have enclosed themselves with their own fat, their mouth hath spoken pride. They that cast me out have now encircled me, they have set their eyes to look askance on the earth. They have taken me as might a lion ready for his prey, and as might a lion's whelp that dwelleth in hiding. Arise, O Lord, overtake them and trip their heels; deliver my soul from ungodly men, Thy sword from the enemies of Thy hand. O Lord, from Thy few do Thou separate them from the earth in their life; yea, with Thy hidden treasures hath their belly been filled. They have satisfied themselves with swine and have left the remnants to their babes. But as for me, in righteousness shall I appear before Thy face; I shall be filled when Thy glory is made manifest to me.

Glory to the Father, and to the Son, and to the Holy Spirit, both now and ever, and unto the ages of ages. Amen.

Alleluia, alleluia, alleluia. Glory to Thee, O God. *Thrice.*

Then, the Small Ectenia:

Deacon (Priest): Again and again, in peace let us pray to the Lord.

CHOIR: Lord, have mercy.

Deacon (Priest): Help us, save us, have mercy on us, and keep us, O God, by Thy grace.

CHOIR: Lord, have mercy.

Deacon (Priest): Calling to remembrance our most holy, most pure, most blessed, glorious Lady Theotokos and Ever-Virgin Mary with all the saints, let us commit ourselves and one another and all our life unto Christ our God.

CHOIR: To Thee, O Lord.

Priest: For Thine is the dominion, and Thine is the kingdom, and the power, and the glory: of the Father, and of the Son, and of the Holy Spirit, now and ever, and unto the ages of ages.

CHOIR: Amen.

Then the Sessional Hymns of the tone or of the feast are read. Then:

CHOIR: Lord, have mercy. *Thrice.* Glory to the Father, and to the Son, and to the Holy Spirit.

Reader: Both now and ever, and unto the ages of ages. Amen.

And the next kathisma is read. On Sundays it is always the 3rd Kathisma. The First Stasis:

PSALM 17

I will love Thee, O Lord, my strength; the Lord is my foundation, and my refuge, and my deliverer. My God is my helper, and I will hope in Him, my defender, and the horn of my salvation, and my helper. With praise will I call upon the name of the Lord, and from mine enemies shall I be saved. The pangs of death surrounded me, and the torrents of iniquity sorely troubled me. The pangs of hades encircled me, round about the snares of death have overtaken me. And in mine affliction I called upon the Lord, and unto my God I cried; He heard my voice out of His holy temple, and my cry before Him shall enter into His ears. And the earth shook and was made to tremble, and the foundations of the mountains were troubled and were shaken, because God was angry with them. There went up smoke in His wrath, and fire from His countenance set all aflame; coals were kindled therefrom. And He bowed the heavens and came down, and thick darkness was under His feet. And He mounted upon cherubim and flew, He flew upon the wings of the winds. And He made darkness His hiding place, His tabernacle round about Him, dark water in the clouds of the air. From the far-shining radiance that was before Him there passed clouds, hail and coals of fire. And the Lord thundered out of heaven, and the Most High gave forth His voice. And He sent forth His arrows, and scattered them; and lightnings He multiplied, and troubled them sorely. And the well-springs of the waters were seen, and the foundations of the world were revealed at Thy rebuke, O Lord, at the on-breathing of the spirit of Thy wrath. He sent from on high, and He took me; He received me out of many waters. He will deliver me from mine enemies which are mighty and from them that hate me, for they are stronger than I. They overtook me in the day of mine affliction, and the Lord became my firm support. And He led me forth into a spacious place; He will deliver me, because He desired me. And the Lord will recompense me according to my righteousness, and according to the purity of my hands will He recompense me. For I have kept the ways of the Lord, and I have not acted impiously toward my God. For all His judgments are before me, and His statutes departed not from me. And I shall be blameless with Him, and I shall keep myself from mine iniquity. And the Lord will reward me according to my righteousness, and according to the purity of my hands before His eyes. With the holy man wilt Thou be holy, and with the innocent man wilt Thou be innocent. And with the elect man wilt Thou be elect, and with the perverse wilt Thou be perverse. For Thou wilt save a humble people, and Thou wilt humble the eyes of the arrogant. For Thou wilt light my lamp, O Lord my God, Thou wilt enlighten my darkness. For by Thee shall I be delivered from a host of robbers, and by my God shall I leap over a wall. As for my God, blameless is His way; the words of the Lord are tried in the fire; defender is He of all that hope in Him. For who is god, save the Lord? And Who is god, save our God? It is God, Who girded me with power, and hath made my path blameless, Who maketh my feet like the feet of a hart, and setteth me upon high places, Who teacheth my hands for war; and Thou madest mine arms a bow of brass. And Thou gavest me the shield of salvation, and Thy right hand hath upheld me. And Thine instruction hath corrected me even unto the end; yea, Thine instruction, the same will teach me. Thou hast enlarged my steps under me, and the tracks of my feet are not weakened. I shall pursue mine enemies and I shall overtake them, and I shall not turn back until they fail. I shall greatly afflict them, and they shall not be able to stand; they shall fall under my feet. For Thou hast girded me with power for war, in subjection under me hast Thou bound the feet of all them that rose up against me. And Thou hast made mine enemies turn their back before me, and them that hate me hast Thou utterly destroyed. They cried, and there was no saviour—even to the Lord, and He hearkened not to them. And I will grind them fine as dust before the face of the wind; I will trample them down as mud in the streets. Deliver me from the gainsaying of the people; Thou wilt set me at the head of nations. A people which I knew not hath served me; no sooner than their ear had heard, they obeyed me. Sons that are stranagers have lied unto me; sons that are strangers have grown old, and they have limped away from their paths. The Lord liveth, and blessed is my God, and let the God of my salvation be exalted. O God Who givest avengement unto me and hast subdued peoples under me, O my Deliverer from enemies which are prone to anger, from them that arise up against me wilt Thou lift me high; from the unrighteous man deliver me. For this cause will I confess Thee among the nations, O Lord, and unto Thy name will I chant. It is He that magnifieth the salvation of His king and worketh mercy for His anointed, for David, and for his seed unto eternity.

Glory to the Father, and to the Son, and to the Holy Spirit.

CHOIR: Both now and ever, and unto the ages of ages. Amen.

Alleluia, alleluia, alleluia. Glory to Thee, O God. *Thrice.* Lord, have mercy. *Thrice.*

Glory to the Father, and to the Son, and to the Holy Spirit.

Reader: Both now and ever, and unto the ages of ages. Amen.

PSALM 18

The heavens declare the glory of God, and the firmament proclaimeth the work of His hands. Day unto day poureth forth speech, and night unto night proclaimeth knowledge. There are no tongues nor words in which their voices are not heard. Their sound hath gone forth into all the earth, and their words unto the ends of the world. In the sun hath He set His tabernacle; and He, like a bridegroom coming forth from his chamber, will rejoice like a giant to run his course. From the outermost border of heaven is His going forth, and His goal is unto the outermost part of heaven, and there shall no man hide himself from His heat. The law of the Lord is blameless, converting souls; the testimony of the Lord is trustworthy, bringing wisdom to infants. The statutes of the Lord are upright, gladdening the heart; the commandment of the Lord is far-shining, enlightening the eyes. The fear of the Lord is pure, enduring for ever and ever; the judgments of the Lord are true, altogether justified, More to be desired than gold and much precious stone, and sweeter than honey and the honeycomb. Yea, for Thy servant keepeth them; in keeping them there is much reward. As for transgressions, who will understand them? From my secret sins cleanse me, and from those of others spare Thy servant. If they have not dominion over me, then blameless shall I be, and I shall be cleansed from great sin. And the sayings of my mouth shall be unto Thy good pleasure, and the meditation of my heart shall be before Thee for ever, O Lord, my helper and redeemer.

PSALM 19

The Lord hear thee in the day of affliction; the name of the God of Jacob defend thee. Let Him send forth unto thee help from His sanctuary, and out of Sion let Him help thee. Let Him remember every sacrifice of thine, and thy whole-burnt offering let Him fatten. The Lord grant thee according to thy heart, and fulfill all thy purposes. We will rejoice in Thy salvation, and in the name of the Lord our God shall we be magnified. The Lord fulfill all thy requests. Now have I known that the Lord hath saved His anointed one; He will hearken unto him out of His holy heaven; in mighty deeds is the salvation of His right hand. Some trust in chariots, and some in horses, but we will call upon the name of the Lord our God. They have been fettered and have fallen, but we are risen and are set upright. O Lord, save the king, and hearken unto us in the day when we call upon Thee.

PSALM 20

O Lord, in Thy strength the king shall be glad, and in Thy salvation shall he rejoice exceedingly. The desire of his heart hast Thou granted unto him, and hast not denied him the requests of his lips. Thou wentest before him with the blessings of goodness, Thou hast set upon his head a crown of precious stone. He asked life of Thee, and Thou gavest him length of days unto ages of ages. Great is his glory in Thy salvation; glory and majesty shalt Thou lay upon him. For Thou shalt give him blessing for ever and ever, Thou shalt gladden him in joy with Thy countenance. For the king hopeth in the Lord, and through the mercy of the Most High shall he not be shaken. Let Thy hand be found on all Thine enemies; let Thy right hand find all that hate Thee. For Thou wilt make them as an oven of fire in the time of Thy presence; the Lord in His wrath will trouble them sorely and fire shall devour them. Their fruit wilt Thou destroy from the earth, and their seed from the sons of men. For they have intended evil against Thee, they have devised counsels which they shall not be able to establish. For Thou shalt make them turn their backs; among those that are Thy remnant, Thou shalt make ready their countenance. Be Thou exalted, O Lord, in Thy strength; we will sing and chant of Thy mighty acts.

Glory to the Father, and to the Son, and to the Holy Spirit.

CHOIR: Both now and ever, and unto the ages of ages. Amen.

Alleluia, alleluia, alleluia. Glory to Thee, O God. *Thrice.* Lord, have mercy. *Thrice.*

Glory to the Father, and to the Son, and to the Holy Spirit.

Reader: Both now and ever, and unto the ages of ages. Amen.

PSALM 21

O God, my God, attend to me; why hast Thou forsaken me? Far from my salvation are the words of my transgressions. My God, I will cry by day, and wilt Thou not hearken? and by night, and it shall not be unto folly for me. But as for Thee, Thou dwellest in the sanctuary, O Praise of Israel. In Thee have our fathers hoped; they hoped, and Thou didst deliver them. Unto Thee they cried, and were saved; in Thee they hoped, and were not brought to shame. But as for me, I am a worm, and not a man, a reproach of men, and the outcast of the people. All that look upon me have laughed me to scorn; they have spoken with their lips and have wagged their heads: He hoped in the Lord; let Him deliver him, let Him save him, for He desireth him. For Thou art He that drewest me forth from the womb; my hope from the breasts of my mother. On Thee was I cast from the womb; from my mother's womb, Thou art my God. Depart not from me, for tribulation is nigh, for there is none to help me. Many bullocks have encircled me, fat bulls have surrounded me. They have opened their mouth against me, as might a lion ravenous and roaring. I have been poured out like water, and scattered are all my bones; my heart is become like wax melting in the midst of my bowels. My strength is dried up like a potsherd, and my tongue hath cleaved to my throat, and into the dust of death hast Thou brought me down. For many dogs have encircled me, the congregation of evildoers hath surrounded me; they have pierced my hands and my feet. They have numbered all my bones, and they themselves have looked and stared upon me. They have parted my garments among themselves, and for my vesture have they cast lots. But Thou, O Lord, remove not Thy help far from me; attend unto mine aid. Rescue my soul from the sword, even this only-begotten one of mine from the hand of the dog. Save me from the mouth of the lion, and my lowliness from the horns of the unicorns. I will declare Thy name unto my brethren, in the midst of the church will I hymn Thee. Ye that fear the Lord, praise Him; all ye that are of the seed of Jacob, glorify Him; let all fear Him that are of the seed of Israel. For He hath not set at nought nor abhorred the supplications of the pauper, nor hath He turned His face from me; and when I cried unto Him, He hearkened unto me. From Thee is my praise; in the great church will I confess Thee; my vows will I pay before them that fear Thee. The poor shall eat and be filled, and they that seek the Lord shall praise Him; their hearts shall live for ever and ever. All the ends of the earth shall remember and shall turn unto the Lord, and all the kindreds of the nations shall worship before Him. For the kingdom is the Lord's and He Himself is sovereign of the nations. All they that be fat upon the earth have eaten and worshipped; all they that go down into the earth shall fall down before Him. Yea, my soul liveth for Him, and my seed shall serve Him. The generation that cometh shall be told of the Lord, and they shall proclaim His righteousness to a people that shall be born, which the Lord hath made.

PSALM 22

The Lord is my shepherd, and I shall not want. In a place of green pasture, there hath He made me to dwell; beside the water of rest hath He nurtured me. He hath converted my soul, He hath led me on the paths of righteousness for His name's sake. For though I should walk in the midst of the shadow of death, I will fear no evil, for Thou art with me;

Thy rod and Thy staff, they have comforted me. Thou hast prepared a table before me in the presence of them that afflict me. Thou hast anointed my head with oil, and Thy cup which filleth me, how excellent it is! And Thy mercy shall pursue me all the days of my life, and I will dwell in the house of the Lord unto length of days.

PSALM 23

The earth is the Lord's, and the fullness thereof, the world, and all that dwell therein. He hath founded it upon the seas, and upon the rivers hath He prepared it. Who shall ascend into the mountain of the Lord? Or who shall stand in His holy place? He that is innocent in hands and pure in heart, who hath not received his soul in vain, and hath not sworn deceitfully to his neighbour. Such a one shall receive a blessing from the Lord, and mercy from God his Saviour. This is the generation of them that seek the Lord, of them that seek the face of the God of Jacob. Lift up your gates, O ye princes; and be ye lifted up, ye everlasting gates, and the King of Glory shall enter in. Who is this King of Glory? The

Lord strong and mighty, the Lord, mighty in war. Lift up your gates, O ye princes; and be ye lifted up, ye everlasting gates, and the King of Glory shall enter in. Who is this King of Glory? The Lord of hosts, He is the King of Glory.

Glory to the Father, and to the Son, and to the Holy Spirit, both now and ever, and unto the ages of ages. Amen.

Alleluia, alleluia, alleluia. Glory to Thee, O God. *Thrice.*

Deacon (Priest): Again and again in peace let us pray to the Lord.

CHOIR: Lord, have mercy.

Deacon (Priest): Help us, save us, have mercy on us, and keep us, O God, by Thy grace.

CHOIR: Lord, have mercy.

Deacon (Priest): Calling to remembrance our most holy, most pure, most blessed, glorious Lady Theotokos and Ever-Virgin Mary with all the saints, let us commit ourselves and one another and all our life unto Christ our God.

CHOIR: To Thee, O Lord.

Priest: For a good God art Thou, and the Lover of mankind, and unto Thee do we send up glory: to the Father, and to the Son, and to the Holy Spirit, now and ever, and unto the ages of ages.

CHOIR: Amen.

And the appointed Sessional Hymns are read.

Then we chant the Polyeleos (Psalms 134 and 135), but usually only the following four verses (the first and last verses of each psalm), on all Sundays from September 21 until December 20 and from January 14 through Cheese-Fare Sunday. Beginning on the First Sunday of Great Lent until the Sunday after September 21, there is no Polyeleos on Sundays, except for Palm Sunday and Pentecost, unless appointed by the Menaion, and we chant the Blameless, i.e., Blessed art Thou, O Lord... *(page 84), immediately after the reading of the Sessional Hymns of the Second Kathisma.*

CHOIR: Praise ye the name of the Lord; O ye servants, praise the Lord. Alleluia, alleluia, alleluia.

Blessed is the Lord out of Sion, Who dwelleth in Jerusalem. Alleluia, alleluia, alleluia.

O give thanks unto the Lord, for He is good; for His mercy endureth for ever. Alleluia, alleluia, alleluia.

O give thanks unto the God of heaven; for His mercy endureth for ever. Alleluia, alleluia, alleluia.

[On the Sunday of the Prodigal Son, Meat-Fare, and Cheese-Fare Sundays, after the Polyeleos we chant Psalm 136: By the rivers of Babylon...*(see Page 141).]*

Then, the megalynarion of the feast is chanted, if there be one, once by the clergy and two or three times by the choir, with the selected psalm verses, and then, after the censing is finished, the clergy chant the megalynarion a final time.

But if it be a Sunday and also a feast of the Theotokos or of a saint having a polyeleos, the megalynarion is chanted only once and only by the clergy, and the choir immediately beginneth to chant the usual Troparia of the Resurrection (i.e., "The Blameless"):

Blessed art Thou, O Lord,* teach me Thy statutes.

The assembly of angels was amazed,* beholding Thee numbered among the dead;* yet, O Saviour,* destroying the stronghold of death,* and with Thyself raising up Adam,* and freeing all from hades.

Blessed art Thou, O Lord,* teach me Thy statutes.

Why mingle ye myrrh with tears of pity,* O ye women disciples?* Thus the radiant angel within the tomb* addressed the myrrh-bearing women;* behold the tomb and understand,* for the Saviour is risen from the tomb.

Blessed art Thou, O Lord,* teach me Thy statutes.

Very early* the myrrh-bearing women hastened* unto Thy tomb, lamenting,* but the angel stood before them and said:* The time for lamentation is passed, weep not,* but tell of the Resurrection to the apostles.

Blessed art Thou, O Lord,* teach me Thy statutes.

The myrrh-bearing women,* with myrrh came to Thy tomb, O Saviour, bewailing,* but the angel addressed them, saying:* Why number ye the living among the dead,* for as God* He is risen from the tomb.

Glory to the Father, and to the Son,* and to the Holy Spirit.

Let us worship the Father,* and His son, and the Holy Spirit,* the Holy Trinity,* one in essence,* crying with the Seraphim:* Holy, Holy, Holy art Thou, O Lord.

Both now and ever,* and unto the ages of ages. Amen.

In bringing forth the Giver of life,* thou hast delivered Adam from sin, O Virgin,* and hast brought joy to Eve* instead of sorrow;* and those fallen from life* have thereunto been restored,* by Him Who of thee was incarnate, God and man.

Alleluia, alleluia, alleluia. Glory to Thee, O God. *Thrice.*

Then the Small Ectenia:

Deacon (Priest): Again and again, in peace let us pray to the Lord.

CHOIR: Lord, have mercy.

Deacon (Priest): Help us, save us, have mercy on us, and keep us, O God, by Thy grace.

CHOIR: Lord, have mercy.

Deacon (Priest): Calling to remembrance our most holy, most pure, most blessed, glorious Lady Theotokos and Ever-Virgin Mary with all the saints, let us commit ourselves and one another and all our life unto Christ our God.

CHOIR: To Thee, O Lord.

Priest: For blessed is Thy name, and glorified is Thy kingdom: of the Father, and of the Son, and of the Holy Spirit, now and ever, and unto the ages of ages.

CHOIR: Amen.

If it be Sunday, the Hypakoe is read (if feasts of the Theotokos or of saints fall on Sunday, their sessional hymns are read after the Hypakoe. Feasts of the Lord which fall on Sunday replace the Octoechos entirely).

Then, on Sundays the Hymns of Ascents of the tone are chanted. On feasts of the Lord and at vigils on other days only the first antiphon of the 4th Tone is chanted, as follows:

CHOIR: From my youth* do many passions war against me;* but do Thou Thyself defend* and save me, O my Saviour.

Ye haters of Sion* shall be shamed by the Lord;* for like grass, by the fire* shall ye be withered.

Glory to the Father, and to the Son,* and to the Holy Spirit,* both now and ever,* and unto the ages of ages. Amen.

In the Holy Spirit,* every soul is quickened,* and, through cleansing, is exalted* and made radiant by the Triple Unity in a hidden holy manner.

Deacon (Priest): Let us attend! Wisdom! Let us attend! The Prokeimenon in the ___ Tone.

And he saith the Prokeimenon of the Sunday tone, or of the feast. The choir chanteth it; he saith the stichos; the choir repeateth the Prokeimenon; he saith the first half or portion (down to the asterisk), and the choir chanteth the remaining portion. On feasts of the Lord or of the Theotokos, regardless of the day of the week, and of saints on other days, the Prokeimenon is always in the 4th Tone.

The Prokeimena for Sunday Matins:

1st Tone: Now will I arise, saith the Lord; I will establish them in salvation,* I will be manifest therein.

Stichos: The words of the Lord are pure words.

2nd Tone: Arouse Thyself, O Lord my God, in the commandment which Thou hast enjoined,* and a congregation of peoples shall surround Thee.

Stichos: O Lord my God, in Thee have I put my hope; save me.

3rd Tone: Say among the nations that the Lord is king; for He hath established the world which shall not be shaken.

Stichos: O sing unto the Lord a new song, sing unto the Lord all the earth.

4th Tone: Arise, O Lord, help us, and redeem us for Thy name's sake.

Stichos: O God, with our ears have we heard, for our fathers have told us.

5th Tone: Arise, O Lord my God, let Thy hand be lifted high; for Thou shalt be king for ever.

Stichos: I will confess Thee, O Lord, with my whole heart, I will tell of all Thy wonders.

6th Tone: O Lord, stir up Thy might and come to save us.

Stichos: O Shepherd of Israel, attend, Thou that leadest Joseph like a sheep.

7th Tone: Arise, O Lord my God, let Thy hand be lifted high; forget not Thy paupers to the end.

Stichos: I will confess Thee, O Lord, with my whole heart, I will tell of all Thy wonders.

8th Tone: The Lord shall be king unto eternity; thy God, O Sion, unto generation and generation.

Stichos: Praise the Lord, O my soul. I will praise the Lord in my life.

Deacon (Priest): Let us pray to the Lord.

CHOIR: Lord, have mercy.

Priest (Bishop): For holy art Thou, O our God, and Thou restest in the saints, and unto Thee do we send up glory: to the Father, and to the Son, and to the Holy Spirit, now and ever, and unto the ages of ages.

CHOIR: Amen.

Deacon (Priest): Let every breath praise the Lord.

CHOIR: Let every breath praise the Lord.

Deacon (Priest): Praise ye God in His saints, praise Him in the firmament of His power.

CHOIR: Let every breath praise the Lord.

Deacon (Priest): Let every breath.

CHOIR: Praise the Lord.

Deacon (Priest): And that He will vouchsafe unto us the hearing of the Holy Gospel, let us pray unto the Lord God.

CHOIR: Lord, have mercy. *Thrice.*

Deacon (Priest): Wisdom! Aright! Let us hear the Holy Gospel.

Priest (Bishop): Peace be unto all.

CHOIR: And to thy spirit.

Priest (Bishop): The Reading is from the Holy Gospel according to *N.*

CHOIR: Glory to Thee, O Lord, glory to Thee.

Deacon (Priest): Let us attend.

And the appointed Gospel is read.

The Eleven Resurrection Gospels

The First Gospel, *Matthew, Section 116 (Chapter 28:16-20), is read on the 1st (8th Tone), 12th (3rd Tone), 23rd (6th Tone), and 34th (1st Tone) Sundays after Pentecost, and on Thomas Sunday.*

At that time, the eleven disciples went away into Galilee, into a mountain where Jesus had appointed them. And when they saw Him, they worshipped Him: but some doubted. And Jesus came and spake unto them, saying, All power is given unto Me in heaven and in earth. Go ye therefore, and teach all nations, baptizing them in the name of the Father, and of the Son, and of the Holy Spirit: teaching them to observe all things whatsoever I have commanded you; and, lo, I am with you alway, even unto the end of the world. Amen.

The Second Gospel, *Mark, Section 70 (Chapter 16:1-8). Read on the 2nd (1st Tone), 13th (4th Tone), 24th (7th Tone), and 35th (2nd Tone)*

Sundays after Pentecost.

At that time, when the sabbath was past, Mary Magdalene, and Mary the mother of James, and Salome, had bought sweet spices, that they might come and anoint Him. And very early in the morning, the first day of the week, they came unto the sepulchre at the rising of the sun. And they said among themselves, Who shall roll us away the stone from the door of the sepulchre? And when they looked, they saw that the stone was rolled away: for it was very great. And entering into the sepulchre, they saw a young man sitting on the right side, clothed in a long white garment; and they were affrighted. And he saith unto them, Be not affrighted: ye seek Jesus of Nazareth, Who was crucified; He is risen; He is not here: behold the place where they laid Him. But go your way, tell His disciples and Peter that He goeth before you into Galilee: there shall ye see Him, as He said unto you. And they went out quickly, and fled from the sepulchre; for they trembled and were amazed; neither said they any thing to any man; for they were afraid. Amen.

The Third Gospel, *Mark, Section 71 (Chapter 16:9-20). Read on the 3rd (2nd Tone), 14th (5th Tone), 25th (8th Tone), and 36th (3rd Tone) Sundays after Pentecost, and on the Sunday of the Myrrh-bearers.*

At that time, when Jesus was risen early the first day of the week, He appeared first to Mary Magdalene, out of whom He had cast seven devils. And she went and told them that had been with Him, as they mourned and wept. And they, when they had heard that He was alive, and had been seen of her, believed not. After that He appeared in another form unto two of them, as they walked, and went into the country. And they went and told it unto the residue: neither believed they them. Afterward He appeared unto the eleven as they sat at table, and upbraided them with their unbelief and hardness of heart, because they believed not them who had seen Him after He was risen. And He said unto them: Go ye into all the world, and preach the Gospel to every creature. He that believeth and is baptized shall be saved; but he that believeth not shall be damned. And these signs shall follow them that believe; In

My name shall they cast out devils; they shall speak with new tongues; they shall take up serpents; and if they drink any deadly thing, it shall not hurt them; they shall lay hands on the sick, and they shall recover. So then, after the Lord had spoken unto them, He ascended up into heaven, and sat on the right hand of God. And they went forth, and preached everywhere, the Lord working with them, and confirming the word with signs following. Amen.

The Fourth Gospel, *Luke, Section 112 (Chapter 24: 1-12). Read on the 4th (3rd Tone), 15th (6th Tone), 26th (1st Tone), and 37th (4th Tone) Sundays, and on the Sunday of the Paralytic.*

At that time, upon the first day of the week, very early in the morning, the women came unto the sepulchre, bringing the spices which they had prepared, and certain others with them. And they found the stone rolled away from the sepulchre. And they entered in, and found not the body of the Lord Jesus. And it came to pass, as they were much perplexed thereabout, behold, two men stood by them in shining garments: and as they were afraid, and bowed down their faces to the earth, they said unto them, Why seek ye the living among the dead? He is not here, but is risen: remember how He spake unto you when He was yet in Galilee, saying, The Son of man must be delivered into the hands of sinful men, and be crucified, and the third day rise again. And they remembered His words, and returned from the sepulchre, and told all these things unto the eleven, and to all the rest. It was Mary Magdalene, and Joanna, and Mary the mother of James, and other women that were with them, who told these things unto the apostles. And their words seemed to them as idle tales, and they believed them not. Then arose Peter, and ran unto the sepulchre; and stooping down, he beheld the linen clothes laid by themselves, and departed, wondering in himself at that which was come to pass. Amen.

The Fifth Gospel, *Luke, Section 113 (Chapter 24:12-35). Read on the 5th (4th Tone), 16th (7th Tone), 27th (2nd Tone), and 38th (5th Tone) Sundays after Pentecost.*

At that time, arose Peter, and ran unto the sepulchre; and stooping down, he beheld the linen clothes laid by themselves, and departed, wondering in himself at that which was come to pass. And behold, two of them went that same day to a village called Emmaus, which was from Jerusalem about threescore furlongs. And they talked together of all these things which had happened. And it came to pass, that while they communed together and reasoned, Jesus Himself drew near, and went with them. But their eyes were holden that they should not know Him. And He said unto them, What manner of communications are these that ye have one to another, as ye walk, and are sad? And one of them, whose name was Cleopas, answering said unto Him, Art thou only a stranger in Jerusalem, and hast not known the things which are come to pass there in these days? And He said unto them, What things? And they said unto Him, Concerning Jesus of Nazareth, Who was a prophet mighty in deed and word before God and all the people; and how the chief priests and our rulers delivered Him to be condemned to death, and have crucified Him. But we trusted that it had been He Who should have redeemed Israel: and beside all this, today is the third day since

these things were done. Yea, and certain
women also of our company made us aston-
ished, who were early at the sepulchre; and
when they found not His body, they came, saying, that they had also seen a vision of angels,
who said that He was alive. And certain of
them that were with us went to the sepulchre,
and found it even so as the women had said:
but Him they saw not. Then He said unto
them: O fools, and slow of heart to believe all
that the prophets have spoken: Ought not
Christ to have suffered these things, and to
enter into His glory? And beginning at Moses
and all the prophets, He expounded unto
them in all the Scriptures the things concerning Himself. And they drew nigh unto the village, whither they went: and He made as
though He would have gone further. But they
constrained Him, saying, Abide with us; for it
is toward evening, and the day is far spent.
And He went in to tarry with them. And it
came to pass, as He sat at table with with them,
He took bread, and blessed it, and brake, and
gave to them. And their eyes were opened,
and they knew Him; and He vanished out of

their sight. And they said one to another, Did not our heart burn within us, while He talked with us by the way, and while He opened to us the Scriptures? And they rose up the same hour, and returned to Jerusalem, and found the eleven gathered together, and them that were with them, saying, The Lord is risen indeed, and hath appeared to Simon. And they told what things were done in the way, and how He was known of them in breaking of bread. Amen.

The Sixth Gospel, *Luke, Section 114 (Chapter 24:36-53). Read on the 6th (5th Tone), 17th (8th Tone), 28th (3rd Tone), and 39th (6th Tone) Sundays.*

At that time, Jesus rose from the dead, stood in the midst of His disciples, and saith unto them: Peace be unto you. But they were terrified and affrighted, and supposed that they had seen a spirit. And He said unto them: Why are ye troubled? and why do thoughts arise in your hearts? Behold My hands and My feet, that it is I Myself: handle Me, and see; for a spirit hath not flesh and bones, as ye see Me have. And when He had thus spoken, He showed them His hands and His feet. And while they yet believed not for joy, and wondered, He said unto them, Have ye here any food? And they gave Him a piece of a broiled fish, and of a honeycomb. And He took it, and did eat before them. And He said unto them: These are the words which I spake unto you, while I was yet with you, that all things must be fulfilled, which were written in the law of Moses, and in the prophets, and in the psalms, concerning Me. Then opened He their understanding, that they might understand the Scriptures, and said unto them, Thus it is written, and thus it behooved Christ to suffer, and to rise from the dead the third day: and that repentance and remission of sins should be preached in His name among all nations, beginning at Jerusalem. And ye are witnesses of these things. And, behold, I send the promise of My Father upon you: but tarry ye in the city of Jerusalem, until ye be endued with power from on high. And He led them out as far as to Bethany, and He lifted up His hands, and blessed them. And it came to pass, while He blessed them, He was parted from them, and carried up into heaven. And they worshipped

Him, and returned to Jerusalem with great joy: and were continually in the temple, praising and blessing God. Amen.

The Seventh Gospel, *John, Section 63 (Chapter 20:1-10). Read on the 7th (6th Tone), 18th (1st Tone), 29th (4th Tone), and 40th (7th Tone) Sundays, and on the Sunday of the Samaritan Woman.*

At that time, on the first day of the week cometh Mary Magdalene early, when it was yet dark, unto the sepulchre, and seeth the stone taken away from the sepulchre. Then she runneth, and cometh to Simon Peter, and to the other disciple, whom Jesus loved, and saith unto them: They have taken away the Lord out of the sepulchre, and I know not where they have laid Him. Peter therefore went forth, and that other disciple, and came to the sepulchre. So they ran both together: and the other disciple did outrun Peter, and came first to the sepulchre. And he stooping down, and looking in, saw the linen clothes lying; yet went he not in. Then cometh Simon Peter following him, and went into the sepulchre, and seeth the linen clothes lie, and the napkin, that was about His head, not lying with the linen clothes, but wrapped together in a place by itself. Then went in also that other disciple, who came first to the sepulchre, and he saw, and believed. For as yet they knew not the Scripture, that He must rise again from the dead. Then the disciples went away again unto their own home. Amen.

The Eighth Gospel, *John, Section 64 (Chapter 20:11-18). Read on the 8th (7th Tone), 19th (2nd Tone), 30th (5th Tone), and 41st (8th Tone) Sundays, and on the Sunday of the Blind Man.*

At that time, Mary stood without at the sepulchre weeping: and as she wept, she stooped down, and looked into the sepulchre, and seeth two angels in white sitting, the one at the head, and the other at the feet, where the body of Jesus had lain. And they say unto her, Woman, why weepest thou? She saith unto them, Because they have taken away my Lord, and I know not where they have laid Him. And when she had thus said, she turned herself back, and saw Jesus standing, and knew not that it was Jesus. Jesus saith unto her, Woman, why weepest thou? whom seekest thou? She, supposing Him to be the gardener, saith unto Him: Sir, if thou have borne Him hence, tell me where thou hast laid Him, and I will take Him away. Jesus saith unto her: Mary. She turned herself, and saith unto Him: Rabboni; which is to say, Master. Jesus saith unto her, Touch Me not; for I am not yet ascended to My Father: but go to My brethren, and say unto them, I ascend unto My Father, and your Father; and to My God, and your God. Mary Magdalene came and told the disciples that she had seen the Lord, and that He had spoken these things unto her. Amen.

The Ninth Gospel, *John, Section 65 (Chapter 20:19-31). Read on the 9th (8th Tone), 20th (3rd Tone), 31st (6th Tone), and 42nd (1st Tone) Sundays.*

At that time, the same day at evening, being the first day of the week, when the doors were shut where the disciples were assembled for fear of the Jews, came Jesus and stood in the midst, and said unto them, Peace be unto you. And when He had so said, He showed unto them His hands and His feet and His side. Then were the disciples glad, when they saw the

Lord. Then said Jesus to them again, Peace be unto you: as My Father hath sent Me, even so send I you. And when He had said this, He breathed on them, and saith unto them, Receive ye the Holy Spirit: whosesoever sins ye remit, they are remitted unto them; and whosesoever sins ye retain, they are retained. But Thomas, one of the twelve, called Didymus, was not with them when Jesus came. The other disciples therefore said unto him, We have seen the Lord. But he said unto them, Except I shall see in His hands the print of the nails, and put my finger into the print of the nails, and thrust my hand into His side, I will not believe. And after eight days again His disciples were within, and Thomas with them: then came Jesus, the doors being shut, and stood in the midst, and said, Peace be unto you. Then saith He to Thomas, Reach hither thy finger, and behold My hands; and reach hither thy hand, and thrust it into My side; and be not faithless, but believing. And Thomas answered and said unto Him, My Lord and my God. Jesus saith unto him, Thomas, because thou hast seen Me, thou hast believed:

blessed are they that have not seen, and yet have believed. And many other signs truly did Jesus in the presence of His disciples, which are not written in this book: but these are written, that ye might believe that Jesus is the Christ, the Son of God; and that believing ye may have life in His name. Amen.

The Tenth Gospel, *John, Section 66 (Chapter 21:1-14). Read on the 10th (1st Tone), 21st (4th Tone), 32nd (7th Tone), and 43rd (2nd Tone) Sundays after Pentecost, and on the 7th Sunday after Pascha, the Sunday of the Holy Fathers.*

At that time, Jesus showed Himself to the disciples at the sea of Tiberias; and on this wise showed He Himself. There were together Simon Peter, and Thomas called Didymus, and Nathanael of Cana in Galilee, and the sons of Zebedee, and two other of His disciples. Simon Peter saith unto them, I go a fishing. They say unto him, We also go with thee. They went forth, and entered into a ship immediately; and that night they caught nothing. But when the morning was now come, Jesus stood on the shore; but the disciples knew not that it was Jesus. Then Jesus saith

unto them, Children, have ye any food? They
answered Him, No. And He said unto them,
Cast the net on the right side of the ship, and
ye shall find. They cast therefore, and now
they were not able to draw it for the multitude
of fishes. Therefore that disciple whom Jesus
loved saith unto Peter, It is the Lord. Now
when Simon Peter heard that it was the Lord,
he girt his fisher's coat unto him (for he was
naked), and did cast himself into the sea. And
the other disciples came in a little ship, (for
they were not far from land, but as it were two
hundred cubits), dragging the net with fishes.
As soon then as they were come to land, they
saw a fire of coals there, and fish laid thereon,
and bread. Jesus saith unto them, Bring of the
fish which ye have now caught. Simon Peter
went up, and drew the net to land full of great
fishes, a hundred and fifty and three: and for
all there were so many, yet was not the net broken. Jesus said unto them: Come and dine.
And none of the disciples durst ask Him, Who
art Thou? knowing that it was the Lord. Jesus
then cometh, and taketh bread, and giveth
them, and fish likewise. This is now the third

time that Jesus showed Himself to His disciples, after that He was risen from the dead. Amen.

The Eleventh Gospel, *John, Section 67 (Chapter 21:14-25). Read on the 11th (2nd Tone), 22nd (5th Tone), 33rd (8th Tone), and 44th (3rd Tone) Sundays after Pentecost.*

At that time, Jesus showed Himself to His disciples after that He was risen from the dead, and said to Simon Peter, Simon, son of Jonas, lovest thou Me more than these? He saith unto Him: Yea, Lord; Thou knowest that I love Thee. He saith unto him, Feed My lambs. He saith to him again the second time, Simon, son of Jonas, lovest thou Me? He said unto Him, Yea, Lord; Thou knowest that I love Thee. He said unto him, Feed My sheep. He said unto him the third time: Simon, son of Jonas, lovest thou Me? Peter was grieved because He said unto him the third time, Lovest thou Me? And he said unto Him, Lord, Thou knowest all things; Thou knowest that I love Thee. Jesus said unto him: Feed My sheep. Amen, amen, I say unto thee, When thou wast young, thou girdedst thyself, and walkedst whither thou wouldest; but when thou shalt be old, thou shalt stretch forth thy hands, and another shall gird thee, and carry thee whither thou wouldest not. This spake He, signifying by what death he should glorify God. And when He had spoken this, He saith unto him, Follow Me. Then Peter, turning about, seeth the disciple whom Jesus loved following; which also leaned on His breast at supper, and said, Lord, which is he that betrayeth Thee? Peter seeing him saith to Jesus, Lord, and what shall this man do? Jesus saith unto him, If I will that he tarry till I come, what is that to thee? follow thou Me. Then went this saying abroad among the brethren, that that disciple should not die: yet Jesus said not unto him, He shall not die; but, if I will that he tarry till I come, what is that to thee? This is the disciple which testifieth of these things, and wrote these things: and I know that his testimony is true. And there are also many other things which Jesus did, the which, if they should be written every one, I suppose that even the world itself could not contain the books that should be written. Amen.

CHOIR: Glory to Thee, O Lord, glory to Thee.

And on Sundays (except Palm Sunday and Pentecost), and on Ascension, and on the Exaltation of the Cross, and on any weekday or Saturday vigil of the Paschal period, we chant once (but on Thomas Sunday and the rest of the Sundays of the Paschal period through the Sunday of the Blind Man, thrice):

CHOIR and People:

Having beheld the Resurrection of Christ,* let us worship the holy Lord Jesus,* the only sinless One.* We worship Thy Cross, O Christ,* and Thy holy Resurrection we hymn and glorify.* For Thou art our God,* and we know none other beside Thee;* we call upon Thy name.* O come, all ye faithful,* let us worship Christ's holy Resurrection,* for, behold, through the Cross joy hath come to all the world.* Ever blessing the Lord,* we hymn His Resurrection;* for, having endured crucifixion,* He hath destroyed death by death.

Then the 50th Psalm is read:

Have mercy on me, O God, according to Thy great mercy; and according to the multitude of Thy compassions blot out my transgression. Wash me thoroughly from mine iniquity, and cleanse me from my sin.

For I know mine iniquity, and my sin is ever before me. Against Thee only have I sinned and done this evil before Thee, that Thou mightest be justified in Thy words, and prevail when Thou art judged. For behold, I was conceived in iniquities, and in sins did my mother bear me. For behold, Thou hast loved truth; the hidden and secret things of Thy wisdom hast Thou made manifest unto me. Thou shalt sprinkle me with hyssop, and I shall be made clean; Thou shalt wash me, and I shall be made whiter than snow. Thou shalt make me to hear joy and gladness; the bones that be humbled, they shall rejoice. Turn Thy face away from my sins, and blot out all mine iniquities. Create in me a clean heart, O God, and renew a right spirit within me. Cast me not away from Thy presence, and take not Thy Holy Spirit from me. Restore unto me the joy of Thy salvation, and with Thy governing Spirit establish me. I shall teach transgressors Thy ways, and the ungodly shall turn back unto Thee. Deliver me from blood-guiltiness, O God, Thou God of my salvation; my tongue shall rejoice in Thy righteousness. O Lord,

Thou shalt open my lips, and my mouth shall declare Thy praise. For if Thou hadst desired sacrifice, I had given it; with whole-burnt offerings Thou shalt not be pleased. A sacrifice unto God is a broken spirit; a heart that is broken and humbled God will not despise. Do good, O Lord, in Thy good pleasure unto Sion, and let the walls of Jerusalem be builded. Then shalt Thou be pleased with a sacrifice of righteousness, with oblation and whole-burnt offerings. Then shall they offer bullocks upon Thine altar.

If it be a feast of the Lord or The Entry of the Theotokos into the Temple, with special stichera, they are chanted here. Otherwise, on Sundays and other vigils we chant in the 6th Tone:

CHOIR: Glory to the Father, and to the Son, and to the Holy Spirit.

Through the prayers of the apostles (*or* the Theotokos, *on her feasts, or* Saint *N., if it be not a Sunday vigil*), O Merciful One,* blot out the multitude of our transgressions.

Both now and ever, and unto the ages of ages. Amen.

Through the prayers of the Theotokos,* O

Merciful One,* blot out the multitude of our transgressions.

Have mercy on me, O God,* according to Thy great mercy;* and according to the multitude of Thy compassions,* blot out my transgression.

And if there be a festal sticheron appointed at this place (for feasts of the Lord and the Theotokos, on any day, including Sundays; for saints, on weekdays only), it is chanted. Otherwise, on Sundays outside of the Lenten cycle we chant:

Jesus having risen from the grave,* as He foretold,* hath give us life eternal,* and great mercy.

But beginning with the Sunday of the Publican and the Pharisee and continuing through the 5th Sunday of Lent, immediately after the 50th Psalm we chant, instead of the preceding verses, the following:

8th Tone: Glory to the Father, and to the Son, and to the Holy Spirit.

The doors of repentance do Thou open to me, O Giver of life,* for my spirit waketh at dawn toward Thy holy temple,* bearing a temple of the body all defiled.* But in Thy compassion cleanse it* by the loving-kindness of Thy mercy.

Both now and ever, and unto the ages of ages. Amen.

Theotokion: Guide me in the paths of salvation, O Theotokos,* for I have defiled my soul with shameful sins,* and have wasted all my life in slothfulness,* but by thine intercessions* deliver me from all uncleanness.

6th Tone: Have mercy on me, O God,* according to Thy great mercy;* and according to the multitude of Thy compassions,* blot out my transgression.

When I think of the multitude of evil things I have done,* I, a wretched one,* I tremble at the fearful day of judgment;* but trusting in the mercy of Thy loving-kindness,* like David do I cry unto Thee:* Have mercy on me, O God,* acccording to Thy great mercy.

Then the deacon (priest) saith:

Save, O God, Thy people, and bless Thine inheritance; visit Thy world with mercy and compassions; exalt the horn of Orthodox Christians, and send down upon us Thine abundant mercies: through the intercessions of our immaculate Lady Theotokos and Ever-Virgin Mary; through the power of the precious and life-giving Cross; through the mediations of the honourable, heavenly Bodiless Hosts; of the honourable, glorious Prophet, Forerunner, and Baptist John; of the holy, glorious, and all-praised apostles; (*if there be commemorated one of the Twelve Apostles or the Evangelists, there is said:* of the holy Apostle (and Evangelist) *N.*, and the other holy, glorious, and all-praised apostles); of our fathers among the saints and great ecumenical teachers and hierarchs: Basil the Great, Gregory the Theologian, and John Chrysostom; of our father among the saints, Nicholas the Wonderworker, archbishop of Myra in Lycia; of the holy Equals-of-the-Apostles Methodius and Cyril, Teachers of the Slavs; of the holy Right-believing and Equal-of-the-Apostles Great Prince Vladimir, and the Blessed Great Princess of Russia Olga; of our fathers among the saints, the Wonderworkers of All Russia: Michael, Peter, Alexius, Jonah, Philip, Macarius, Demetrius, Metrophanes, Tikhon, Theodosius, Joasaph, Hermogenes, Pitirim,

Innocent, and John; of the holy Hieromartyrs and Confessors: Tikhon, Patriarch of Moscow; the Metropolitans: Vladimir of Kiev, Benjamin and Joseph of Petrograd, Peter of Krutitsa, Cyril of Kazan, Agathangel of Yaroslavl; Andronicus of Perm, Hermogenes of Tobolsk, the priests John, John, Peter, and Philosoph, and all the new hieromartyrs and confessors of the Russian Church; of the holy, glorious, and victorious martyrs: the holy, glorious Great-martyr, Trophy-bearer, and Wonderworker George; the holy Great-martyr and Healer Panteleimon; the holy Great-martyr Barbara; and the holy Right-believing Russian Princes and Passion-bearers Boris and Gleb, and Igor; and the holy Passion-bearers: Tsar-martyr Nicholas, Tsaritsa-martyr Alexandra, the Martyred Crown Prince Alexius, the Royal Martyrs Olga, Tatiana, Maria, and Anastasia; and the holy nun-martyrs: Grand Duchess Elizabeth and Nun Barbara, and all the New Martyrs of Russia; of our holy and God-bearing fathers Anthony and Theodosius of the Kiev Caves; Sergius, the Abbot of Radonezh, and Seraphim of Sarov; Job, Abbot and Wonderworker of Pochaev; of the holy Righteous John of Kronstadt; of the holy Blessed Xenia; of our holy and God-bearing fathers: Herman of Alaska; Paisius Velichkovsky; Leo, Macarius, Ambrose, and the other Elders of Optina; the hierarchs Innocent of Moscow, Nicholas of Japan, John of Shanghai and San Francisco; and Saint(s) *N.(N.), (whose temple it is and whose day it is)* whose memory we celebrate; of the holy and Righteous Ancestors of God Joachim and Anna; and of all the saints; we pray Thee, O Lord plenteous in mercy, hearken unto us sinners that pray unto Thee, and have mercy on us.

CHOIR: Lord, have mercy. *Twelve times.*

Priest (Bishop): Through the mercy and compassions and love for mankind of Thine Only-begotten Son, with Whom Thou art blessed, together with Thy Most-holy and good and life-creating Spirit, now and ever, and unto the ages of ages.

CHOIR: Amen.

And the appointed canons are read.

And the clergy and the people venerate the Gospel and/or the icon of the feast, and receive anointing with oil (and, if there was a Litia, a piece of the bread moistened with the wine blessed at the Litia).

After the 3rd Ode of the canons, the Small Ectenia:

Deacon (Priest): Again and again, in peace let us pray to the Lord.

CHOIR: Lord, have mercy.

Deacon (Priest): Help us, save us, have mercy on us, and keep us, O God, by Thy grace.

CHOIR: Lord, have mercy.

Deacon (Priest): Calling to remembrance our most holy, most pure, most blessed, glorious Lady Theotokos and Ever-Virgin Mary with all the saints, let us commit ourselves and one another and all our life unto Christ our God.

CHOIR: To Thee, O Lord.

Priest: For Thou art our God, and unto Thee do we send up glory: to the Father, and to the Son, and to the Holy Spirit, now and ever, and unto the ages of ages.

CHOIR: Amen.

Then the sessional hymns and/or kontakion as appointed. After the 6th Ode of the canons, again the Small Ectenia (see preceding page), with the following exclamation:

Priest: For Thou art the King of Peace and the Saviour of our souls, and unto Thee do we send up glory: to the Father, and to the Son, and to the Holy Spirit, now and ever, and unto the ages of ages.

CHOIR: Amen.

Then the resurrectional kontakion and ekos of the tone (or of the Holy Fathers on Sundays when they are commemorated), or of the feast.

After the 8th Ode of the canons we chant:

CHOIR: We praise, we bless, we worship the Lord, praising and supremely exalting Him unto all ages. *And then the katavasia.*

Deacon (Priest): The Theotokos and Mother of the Light let us magnify in song.

And we chant the Song of the Most Holy Theotokos (the Magnificat) (on great feasts special megalynaria are chanted instead of the Magnificat):

CHOIR: My soul doth magnify the Lord,* and my spirit hath rejoiced in God my Saviour.

And after each verse the refrain: More honourable than the Cherubim,* and beyond compare more glorious than the Seraphim,* who without corruption gavest birth to God the Word,* the very Theotokos, thee do we magnify.

For He hath looked upon the lowliness of His handmaiden;* for behold, from henceforth all generations shall call me blessed. *Refrain.*

For the Mighty One hath done great things to me,* and holy is His name; and His mercy is on them that fear Him unto generation and generation. *Refrain.*

He hath showed strength with His arm,* and He hath scattered the proud in the imagination of their heart. *Refrain.*

He hath put down the mighty from their seat,* and exalted them of low degree;* He hath filled the hungry with good things,* and the rich He hath sent empty away. *Refrain.*

He hath holpen His servant Israel* in remembrance of His mercy,* as He spake to our fathers,* to Abraham and his seed for ever. *Refrain.*

Then the 9th Ode of the canons. After the 9th Ode, and the katavasia, again the Small Ectenia:

Deacon (Priest): Again and again, in peace let us pray to the Lord.

CHOIR: Lord, have mercy.

Deacon (Priest): Help us, save us, have mercy on us, and keep us, O God, by Thy grace.

CHOIR: Lord, have mercy.

Deacon (Priest): Calling to remembrance

our most holy, most pure, most blessed, glorious Lady Theotokos and Ever-Virgin Mary with all the saints, let us commit ourselves and one another and all our life unto Christ our God.

CHOIR: To Thee, O Lord.

Priest: For all the Hosts of Heaven praise Thee, and unto Thee do we send up glory: to the Father, and to the Son, and to the Holy Spirit, now and ever, and unto the ages of ages.

CHOIR: Amen.

Then, if it be Sunday (but not on Pascha, Pentecost, or any Sunday coinciding with Transfiguration or the Exaltation of the Cross):

Deacon (Priest): Holy is the Lord our God.

CHOIR: Holy is the Lord our God.

Stichos: For holy is the Lord our God.

CHOIR: Holy is the Lord our God.

Stichos: Above all peoples is our God.

CHOIR: Holy is the Lord our God.

After this, the Exaposteilaria of the Resurrection and/or the feast.

Then Lauds (the Praises) in the tone of the Sunday or of the feast. CHOIR:

Let every breath praise the Lord.* Praise the Lord from the heavens,* praise Him in the highest.* To Thee is due praise, O God.

Praise Him, all ye His angels;* praise Him, all ye His hosts.* To Thee is due praise, O God.

Then, straight chant on one note, as on "do," going up one step on the next-to-the-last word(s) or syllable(s) and back down again on the last stressed word(s) or syllable(s). The word(s) or syllable(s) which should be raised one note are in boldface type. Also, the verses may be read down to To do among them the judgment that is written, *page 122.*

Praise Him, O sun and moon; praise Him, all ye **stars and** light.

Praise Him, ye heavens of heavens, and thou water that art above the **heav**-ens.

Let them praise the name of the Lord; for He spake, and they came to be; He commanded, and they were cre-**at**-ed.

He established them for ever, yea, for ever and ever; He hath set an ordinance, and it shall not **pass a**-way.

Praise the Lord from the earth, ye dragons and all ye a-**byss**-es.

Fire, hail, snow, ice, blast of tempest, which per-**form His** word.

The mountains and all the hills, fruitful trees, and all **ce**-dars.

The beasts and all the cattle, creeping things and **wing-ed** birds.

Kings of the earth, and all peoples, princes and all **judges of the** earth.

Young men and virgins, elders with the younger; let them praise the name of the Lord, for exalted is the name of **Him** a-lone.

His praise is above the earth and heaven, and He shall exalt the horn of His **peo**-ple.

This is the hymn for all His saints, for the sons of Israel, and for the people that draw **nigh unto** Him.

Sing unto the Lord a new song; His praise is in the **church of the** saints.

Let Israel be glad in Him that made him, let the name of Sion re-**joice in their** king.

Let them praise His name in the dance; with the timbrel and the psaltery let them **chant unto** Him.

For the Lord taketh pleasure in His people, and He shall exalt the meek with sal-**va**-tion.

The saints shall boast in glory, and they shall re-**joice upon their** beds.

The high praise of God shall be in their throat, and two-edged swords shall **be in their** hands.

To do vengeance among the heathen, punishments among the **peo**-ples.

To bind their kings with fetters, and their nobles with manacles of **i**-ron.

If there be 6 stichera appointed:

Reader/Canonarch: (Prosomion: ___, *if there be one)* To do among them the judgment that is written.

CHOIR: This glory shall be to all His saints. *And the first sticheron.*

Praise ye God in His saints,* praise Him in the firmament of His power. *Sticheron.*

If there be 4 stichera appointed:

Praise Him for His mighty acts,* praise Him according to the multitude of His greatness. *Sticheron.*

Praise Him with the sound of trumpet,* praise Him with psaltery and harp. *Sticheron.*

Praise Him with timbrel and dance,* praise Him with strings and flute. *Sticheron.*

Praise Him with tuneful cymbals, praise Him with cymbals of jubilation.* Let every breath praise the Lord. *Sticheron.*

On Sundays, when there is always a minimum of 8 stichera appointed, these two stichoi are added:

Arise, O Lord my God, let Thy hand be lifted high;* forget not Thy paupers to the end. *Sticheron.*

I will confess Thee, O Lord, with my whole heart,* I will tell of all Thy wonders. *Sticheron.*

Reader/Canonarch: Glory in the ___ Tone.

CHOIR: Glory to the Father, and to the Son, and to the Holy Spirit.

If it be a Sunday, the Gospel sticheron is chanted, unless there be a Doxastichon from the Menaion, the Triodion, or the Pentecostarion.

Both now and ever, and unto the ages of ages. Amen.

Theotokion, 2nd Tone: Most blessed art Thou, O Virgin Theotokos, * for through Him Who became incarnate of thee is hades led captive,* Adam recalled, the curse annulled, Eve set free,* death slain, and we are given life.* Wherefore, we cry aloud in praise:* Blessed is Christ God Who hast been so pleased, glory to Thee.

Priest (Bishop): Glory to Thee Who hast

showed us the light.

CHOIR:

G lory to God in the highest, and on earth peace, good will among men. We praise Thee, we bless Thee, we worship Thee, we glorify Thee, we give thanks to Thee for Thy great glory. O Lord, Heavenly King, God the Father Almighty; O Lord, the Only-begotten Son, Jesus Christ; and O Holy Spirit. O Lord God, Lamb of God, Son of the Father, that takest away the sin of the world, have mercy on us; Thou that takest away the sins of the world, receive our prayer; Thou that sittest at the right hand of the Father, have mercy on us. For Thou only art Holy, Thou only art the Lord, Jesus Christ, to the glory of God the Father. Amen.

Every day will I bless Thee, and I will praise Thy name for ever, yea, for ever and ever.

Vouchsafe, O Lord, to keep us this day without sin. Blessed art Thou, O Lord, the God of our fathers, and praised and glorified is Thy name unto the ages. Amen.

Let Thy mercy, O Lord, be upon us, according as we have hoped in Thee.

Blessed art Thou, O Lord, teach me Thy statutes. *Thrice.*

Lord, Thou hast been our refuge in generation and generation. I said: O Lord, have mercy on me, heal my soul, for I have sinned against Thee.

O Lord, unto Thee have I fled for refuge, teach me to do Thy will, for Thou art my God; for in Thee is the fountain of life, in Thy light shall we see light. O continue Thy mercy unto them that know Thee.

Holy God, Holy Mighty, Holy Immortal, have mercy on us. *Thrice.*

Glory to the Father, and to the Son, and to the Holy Spirit, both now and ever, and unto the ages of ages. Amen.

Holy Immortal, have mercy on us.

Holy God, Holy Mighty, Holy Immortal, have mercy on us.

If it be a Sunday and a feast of the Lord coincide, we chant the troparion of the feast. If it be a vigil on any other day of the week, we chant the troparion of the feast. But if it be a regular Sunday, even if a feast of the Theotokos or a saint coincide, we chant one of the following troparia.

If it be a 1st, 3rd, 5th, or 7th Tone Sunday, we chant in the **1st Tone:**

Today is salvation come unto the world;* let us sing praises to Him that arose from the tomb,* and is the Author of our life.* For, having destroyed death by death,* He hath given us the victory and great mercy.

If it be a 2nd, 4th, 6th, or 8th Tone Sunday, we chant in the **2nd Tone:**

Having risen from the tomb, and having burst the bonds of hades,* Thou hast destroyed the sentence of death, O Lord,* delivering all from the snares of the enemy.* Manifesting Thyself to Thine apostles, Thou didst send them forth to preach;* and through them hast granted Thy peace to the world,* O Thou Who alone art plenteous in mercy.

Then the Ecteniae.

Deacon (Priest): Have mercy on us, O God, according to Thy great mercy, we pray Thee, hearken and have mercy.

CHOIR: Lord, have mercy. *Thrice. And likewise for the remaining petitions.*

Deacon (Priest): Again we pray for the Orthodox episcopate of the Church of Russia; for our lord the Very Most Reverend Metropolitan *N.*, First Hierarch of the Russian Church Abroad; for our lord the Most Reverend (Archbishop *or* Bishop *N., whose diocese it is*); and for all our brethren in Christ.

Again we pray for the suffering Russian land and its Orthodox people both in the homeland and in the diaspora, and for their salvation.

Again we pray for this land, its authorities and armed forces.

Again we pray to the Lord our God that He may deliver His people from enemies visible and invisible, and confirm in us oneness of mind, brotherly love, and piety.

Again we pray for the blessed and evermemorable founders of this holy temple (*or* monastery, *or* convent), and for all our fathers and brethren gone to their rest before us, and the Orthodox here and everywhere laid to rest.

Again we pray for mercy, life, peace, health, salvation, visitation, pardon and remission of the sins of the servants of God, the brethren of this holy temple (*or* monastery).

Again we pray for them that bring offerings

and do good works in this holy and all-venerable temple; for them that minister and them that chant, and for all the people here present, that await of Thee great and abundant mercy.

CHOIR: Lord, have mercy. *Thrice.*

Priest: For a merciful God art Thou, and the Lover of mankind, and unto Thee do we send up glory: to the Father, and to the Son, and to the Holy Spirit, now and ever, and unto the ages of ages.

CHOIR: Amen.

Deacon (Priest): Let us complete our morning prayer unto the Lord.

CHOIR: Lord, have mercy.

Deacon (Priest): Help us, save us, have mercy on us, and keep us, O God, by Thy grace.

CHOIR: Lord, have mercy.

Deacon (Priest): That the whole evening may be perfect, holy, peaceful, and sinless, let us ask of the Lord.

CHOIR: Grant this, O Lord. *And also after the next five petitions.*

Deacon (Priest): An angel of peace, a faithful guide, a guardian of our souls and bodies, let us ask of the Lord.

Pardon and remission of our sins and offences, let us ask of the Lord.

Things good and profitable for our souls, and peace for the world, let us ask of the Lord.

That we may complete the remaining time of our life in peace and repentance, let us ask of the Lord.

A Christian ending to our life, painless, blameless, peaceful, and a good defence before the dread judgment seat of Christ, let us ask.

Calling to remembrance our most holy, most pure, most blessed, glorious Lady Theotokos and Ever-Virgin Mary with all the saints, let us commit ourselves and one another and all our life unto Christ our God.

CHOIR: To Thee, O Lord.

Priest: For Thou art a God of mercy, compassion, and love for mankind, and unto Thee do we send up glory: to the Father, and to the Son, and to the Holy Spirit, now and ever, and unto the ages of ages.

CHOIR: Amen.

Priest: Peace be unto all.

CHOIR: And to thy spirit.

Deacon (Priest): Let us bow our heads unto the Lord.

CHOIR: To Thee, O Lord.

Priest: For Thine it is to show mercy and to save us, O our God, and unto Thee do we send up glory: to the Father, and to the Son, and to the Holy Spirit, now and ever, and unto the ages of ages.

CHOIR: Amen.

Deacon (Priest): Wisdom!

CHOIR: Bless (*or:* Master, bless).

Priest (Bishop): He that is is blessed, Christ our God, always, now and ever, and unto the ages of ages.

CHOIR: Amen. Establish, O God, the holy Orthodox Faith of Orthodox Christians unto the ages of ages.

Priest (Bishop): O most holy Theotokos, save us.

CHOIR: More honourable than the Cherubim, and beyond compare more glorious than the Seraphim, who without corruption gavest birth to God the Word, the very Theotokos, thee do we magnify.

Priest (Bishop): Glory to Thee, O Christ

God, our hope, glory to Thee.

CHOIR: Glory to the Father, and to the Son, and to the Holy Spirit, both now and ever, and unto the ages of ages. Amen.

Lord, have mercy. *Thrice.* (Master) Bless.

Priest (Bishop): May Christ our true God (*Sundays:* Who rose from the dead), through the intercessions of His most pure Mother, (*Sundays:* of the holy, glorious, and all-praised apostles), and *Saint(s) N.(N.), (whose temple it is and whose day it is);* of the holy and Righteous Ancestors of God Joachim and Anna, and of all the saints, have mercy on us and save us, for He is good and the Lover of mankind.

CHOIR: Amen. The Orthodox episcopate of the Church of Russia;* our lord the Very Most Reverend Metropolitan *N.,* First Hierarch of the Russian Church Abroad;* and our lord the Most Reverend (Archbishop *or* Bishop *N.*);* the brotherhood of this holy temple (*or* monastery, *or* community, *or* sisterhood of this holy convent, *etc.*), and all Orthodox Christians,* preserve, O Lord, for MANY YEARS!

AND THE FIRST HOUR IS READ

❊❊❊❊❊❊❊

THE FIRST HOUR

Reader: O come, let us worship God our King.

O come, let us worship and fall down before Christ our King and God.

O come, let us worship and fall down before Christ Himself, our King and God.

PSALM 5

Unto my words give ear, O Lord; hear my cry. Attend unto the voice of my supplication, O my King and my God; for unto Thee will I pray, O Lord. In the morning Thou shalt hear my voice. In the morning shall I stand before Thee, and Thou shalt look upon me; for not a God that willest iniquity art Thou. He that worketh evil shall not dwell near Thee, nor shall transgressors abide before Thine eyes. Thou hast hated all them that work iniquity; Thou shalt destroy all them that speak a lie. A man that is bloody and deceitful shall the Lord abhor. But as for me, in the multitude of Thy mercy shall I go into Thy house; I shall worship toward Thy holy temple in fear of Thee. O Lord, guide me in the way of Thy righteousness; because of mine enemies, make straight my way before Thee. For in their mouth there is no truth; their heart is vain. Their throat is an open sepulchre, with their tongues have they spoken deceitfully; judge them, O God. Let them fall down on account of their own devisings; according to the multitude of their ungodliness, cast them out, for they have embittered Thee, O Lord. And let all them be glad that hope in Thee; they shall ever rejoice, and Thou shalt dwell among them. And all shall glory in Thee that love Thy name, for Thou shalt bless the righteous. O Lord, as with a shield of Thy good pleasure hast Thou crowned us.

PSALM 89

Lord, Thou hast been our refuge in generation and generation. Before the mountains came to be and the earth was formed and the world, even from everlasting to everlasting Thou art. Turn not man away unto lowliness; yea, Thou hast said: Turn back, ye sons of men. For a thousand years in Thine eyes, O Lord, are but as yesterday that is past, and as a watch in the night. Things of no account shall their years be; in the morning like grass shall man pass away. In the morning shall he bloom and pass away, in the evening shall he fall and grow withered and dry. For we have fainted away in Thy wrath and in Thine anger have we been troubled. Thou hast set our iniquities before Thee; our lifespan is in the light of Thy countenance. For all our days are faded away, and in the Thy wrath are we fainted away; our years have, like a spider, spun out their tale. As for the days of our years, in their span they be threescore years and ten. And if we be in strength, mayhap fourscore years; and what is more than these is toil and travail. For mildness is come upon us, and we shall be chastened. Who knoweth the might of Thy wrath? And out of fear of Thee, who can recount Thine anger? So make Thy right hand known to me, and to them that in their heart are instructed in wisdom. Return, O Lord; how long? And be Thou entreated concerning Thy servants. We were filled in the morning with Thy mercy, O Lord, and we rejoiced and were glad. In all our days, let us be glad for the days wherein Thou didst humble us, for the years wherein we saw evils. And look upon Thy servants, and upon Thy works, and do Thou guide their sons. And let the brightness of the Lord our God be upon us, and the works of our hands do Thou guide aright upon us, yea, the work of our hands do Thou guide aright.

PSALM 100

Of mercy and judgment will I sing unto Thee, O Lord; I will chant and have understanding in a blameless path. When wilt Thou come unto me? I have walked in the innocence of my heart in the midst of my house. I have no unlawful thing before mine eyes; the workers of transgressions I have hated. A crooked heart hath not cleaved unto me; as for the wicked man who turned from me, I knew him not. Him that privily talked against his neighbour did I drive away from me. With him whose eye was proud and his heart insatiate, I did not eat. Mine eyes were upon the faithful of the land, that they might sit with me; the man that walked in the blameless path, he ministered unto me. The proud doer dwelt not in the midst of my house; the speaker of unjust things prospered not before mine eyes. In the morning I slew all the sinners of the land, utterly to destroy out of the city of the Lord all them that work iniquity.

Glory to the Father, and to the Son, and to the Holy Spirit, both now and ever, and unto the ages of ages. Amen.

Alleluia, alleluia, alleluia. Glory to Thee, O God. *Thrice.* Lord, have mercy. *Thrice.*

Here we say the first troparion, if there be two. If not, we continue with:

Glory to the Father, and to the Son, and to the Holy Spirit. *And the second troparion, if any. If not, the only troparion. Then:*

Both now and ever, and unto the ages of ages. Amen. **Theotokion:**

What shall we call thee, O thou that art full of grace? Heaven: for thou hast dawned forth the Sun of Righteousness. Paradise: for thou hast blossomed forth the Flower of Immortality. Virgin: for thou hast remained incorrupt. Pure Mother: for thou hast held in thy holy embrace the Son, the God of all. Do thou entreat Him to save our souls.

My steps do Thou direct according to Thy saying, and let no iniquity have dominion over me. Deliver me from the false accusation of men, and I will keep Thy commandments. Make Thy face to shine upon Thy servant, and teach me Thy statutes.

Let my mouth be filled with Thy praise, O Lord, that I may hymn Thy glory and Thy majesty all the day long.

Holy God, Holy Mighty, Holy Immortal, have mercy on us. *Thrice.*

Glory to the Father, and to the Son, and to the Holy Spirit, both now and ever, and unto the ages of ages. Amen.

O Most Holy Trinity, have mercy on us. O Lord, blot out our sins. O Master, pardon our iniquities. O Holy One, visit and heal our infirmities for Thy name's sake.

Lord, have mercy. *Thrice.*

Glory to the Father, and to the Son, and to the Holy Spirit, both now and ever, and unto the ages of ages. Amen.

Our Father, Who art in the heavens, hallowed be Thy name. Thy kingdom come, Thy will be done, on earth as it is in heaven. Give us this day our daily bread; and forgive us our debts, as we forgive our debtors; and lead us not into temptation, but deliver us from the evil one.

Priest: For Thine is the kingdom, and the power, and the glory: of the Father, and of the Son, and of the Holy Spirit, now and ever, and unto the ages of ages.

Reader: Amen. *And he saith the kontakion. If there be two kontakia, he readeth the kontakion that was chanted after the 3rd Ode of the canons at Matins.*

Then: Lord, have mercy. *Forty times.*

And the Prayer of the Hours:

Thou Who at all times and at every hour, in heaven and on earth, art worshipped and glorified, O Christ God, Who art long-suffering, plenteous in mercy, most compassionate, Who lovest the righteous and hast mercy on sinners, Who callest all to salvation through the promise of good things to come: Receive, O Lord, our prayers at this hour, and guide our life toward Thy commandments. Sanctify our souls, make chaste our bodies, correct our thoughts, purify our intentions, and deliver us from every sorrow, evil, and pain. Compass us about with Thy holy angels, that, guarded and guided by their array, we may attain to the unity of the faith, and the knowledge of Thine unapproachable glory; for blessed art Thou unto the ages of ages. Amen.

Lord, have mercy. *Thrice.*

Glory to the Father, and to the Son, and to the Holy Spirit, both now and ever, and unto the ages of ages. Amen.

More honourable than the Cherubim, and beyond compare more glorious than the Seraphim, who without corruption gavest birth to God the Word, the very Theotokos, thee do we magnify.

In the name of the Lord, father (master), bless.

Priest: God be gracious unto us and bless us, and cause Thy face to shine upon us and have mercy on us.

Reader: Amen.

Priest, the Prayer of the First Hour:

O Christ the True Light, Who enlightenest and sanctifiest every man that cometh into the world: Let the light of Thy countenance be signed upon us, that in it we may see the Unapproachable Light, and guide our steps in the doing of Thy commandments, through the intercessions of Thy most pure Mother, and of all Thy saints. Amen.

CHOIR, **8th Tone:** To thee, the Champion Leader, we thy servants dedicate a feast of victory and of thanksgiving* as ones rescued out of sufferings, O Theotokos;* but as thou art one with might which is invincible,* from all dangers that can be do thou deliver us, that we may cry to thee:* Rejoice! thou Bride Unwedded.

Priest: Glory to Thee, O Christ God, our hope, glory to Thee.

CHOIR: Glory to the Father, and to the Son, and to the Holy Spirit, both now and ever, and unto the ages of ages. Amen.

Lord, have mercy. *Thrice.* Father (Master), bless.

Priest, the dismissal: May Christ our true God (*Sundays:* Who rose from the dead), through the intercessions of His most pure Mother, of our holy and God-bearing fathers, and of all the saints, have mercy on us and save us, for He is good and the Lover of mankind.

CHOIR: Amen. Lord, have mercy. *Thrice.*

THE END OF THE ALL-NIGHT VIGIL

✾✾✾✾✾✾✾✾

On the Sunday of the Prodigal Son, and on Meat-Fare and Cheese-Fare Sundays, the 136th Psalm is chanted after the Polyeleos, page 84:

By the rivers of Babylon, there we sat down and we wept when we remembered Sion. Alleluia.

Upon the willows in the midst thereof did we hang our instruments. Alleluia.

For there, they that had taken us captive asked us for words of song. And they that had led us away asked us for a hymn. Alleluia.

Saying: Sing us one of the songs of Sion. Alleluia.

How shall we sing the Lord's song in a strange land? Alleluia.

If I forget thee, O Jerusalem, let my right hand be forgotten. Alleluia.

Let my tongue cleave to my throat, if I remember thee not. Alleluia.

If I set not Jerusalem above all other, as at the head of my joy. Alleluia.

Remember, O Lord, the sons of Edom, in the day of Jerusalem, who said: Lay waste, lay waste to her, even to the foundations thereof. Alleluia.

O daughter of Babylon, thou wretched one, blessed shall he be who shall reward thee wherewith thou hast rewarded us. Alleluia.

Blessed shall he be who shall seize and dash thine infants against the rock. Alleluia.

———————————————